Spirit Movers

Spirit Movers

Attributes for Transforming Leadership

CILE CHAVEZ & JULIE REDER FAIRLEY

New York

Spirit Movers
Attributes for Transforming Leadership

Softcover ISBN: 978-1-60037-739-6

Hardcover ISBN: 978-1-60037-740-2

Library of Congress Control Number: 2009942860

Morgan James Publishing
1225 Franklin Ave., STE 325
Garden City, NY 11530-1693
Toll Free 800-485-4943
www.MorganJamesPublishing.com

Contents

Dedication

For all they have been;
all they have borne;
all they have become;
and all they have yet to be,
we dedicate this book:

To our children:
Brian Chavez, Mark Chavez, Julie Marie Chavez Cerbo,
Evelyn Fairley O'Dwyer, and Mark Howard Fairley

And their children:
Mattea Marie Cerbo, Sienna Marie Cerbo,
Brendan Fairley O'Dwyer, Mairead Teagan O'Dwyer,
and the gifts of posterity yet to come.

Acknowledgments

We are grateful:

- To those who have given us opportunities to serve in leadership positions. The roles with which you entrusted us inspired our hearts and informed our minds.
- To all the teachers, mentors, colleagues, friends, and family who have guided us in a spirit way of leadership. We hope you see your reflection in our book.
- To our clients in the private and public sectors. We are grateful for your feedback and validation of the merits of our work.
- To Curt Coffman, author and supporter, who, without reservation, said yes to the promise of our book. The gift of his foreword to this book is accepted with deep appreciation.
- To those who know our hearts and heard our voices long before the written word, we say thank you.

With significance we recognize and honor three gifted advisors who were unselfish with their time, critical in their analysis, committed to excellence, and loving in spirit:

Mary Jarvis, Ed.D: The *encourager*—who urged us to commit thoughts to paper, was unwavering in support, and celebrated the merits of our collaboration.

Elliot Asp, PhD: The *guide*—who brought clarity to our framework of a rubric for examining the facets of leadership.

Margaret Hatcher Ed.D: The *sage*—who elevated our thinking and deepened our own appreciation for the concept of spirit movers. The *artist* who gifted us with a remarkable painting for the cover, reflecting our intentions.

We are frequently asked, *"How was it writing a book with someone else?"* Our collective voice replies, "Joyful!" And so, we thank each other for the gifts of intellectual rigor, creative energies, playful words, commitment to hard work, and a caring friendship that sustained our vision.

Foreword

Frankly, I'm tired of books about leadership. For the last twenty years, you'd think there had been no other important business topics. Funny, though—when I look at the current economic climate, the calamity is mostly the result of very bad leadership. Think about it—after billions of dollars spent on leadership development, we're still in the midst of a mess resulting from misguided, selfish, and short-sighted direction.

Don't get me wrong—I am all for leadership improvement. However, let's be truthful. In our quest for it, we have somehow gone astray. Everyone seems to be seeking a magic formula for extraordinary leadership. In our efforts to package this formula, we have come up with ideal behaviors that everyone is encouraged to adopt. However, we're not lead to developing leaders—we're creating Frankenstein! We claim that leaders should have a little of this (strategic thinking), a little of that (calm under fire), and twenty-three other characteristics. We then evaluate the strength or weakness of these critical traits and judge an individual's leadership aptitude. How arrogant!

One of the problems with this conventional competency approach is the challenge of evaluation. If someone possesses twelve of the twenty-five checklist attributes this year and seventeen the following year, has that person's performance significantly improved? Worse yet, just maybe the evaluation of the competencies reflects the evaluator's views and perceptions more than the actual performance of the person under review! While this approach provides a common language and is easy to teach, the consequences on organizations, not to mention individuals, have been detrimental.

If you're looking for that approach, put this book down and walk away! In these pages you will be challenged to fully examine yourself first and how you influence others second. The authors don't even attempt to show you the way. Rather; they take you on a journey of self-discovery.

True leadership growth starts with the realization that it is about the outcomes, not how you "do" it. Every leader needs to be a fully aware and functioning person first. This is the greatest challenge for leaders. Effective leadership is a result of understanding how you influence others, build relationships, and get things done and most importantly, how you keep relationships growing and expanding.

A book isn't solely words and pages, but a heart exposed by its authors. Cile and Julie are this book. They have shared a lifelong passion for helping others perform at their highest levels as students, parents, teachers, managers, leaders, and, yes, human beings. They have discovered the fibers of a fabric that is the true model of leadership and impact.

Their challenge for examination is on every page and unfortunately some are not yet ready to embrace this challenge. But if you give it a chance, you will walk away with a tapestry of self-understanding to be appreciated versus one that needs to be changed. Through the discovery of your unique pattern, you will be able to embrace and employ your talents and uniqueness fully in order to have unbelievable impact upon the world and the people in it.

Curt Coffman
Author, Researcher, Consultant, Speaker
The Coffman Organization
Denver, Colorado

Introduction

The Invitation

I n a world depending on leadership for its very continuance, there is a constant demand for intelligent, compassionate, courageous leaders. The burdens on those who would champion the causes of organizations for a better society are both never ending and ever changing. Our intention is to offer all who have a passion for leadership an invitation to follow the words of the French poet Guillaume Apollinaire, who wrote:

> *"Come to the edge," he said.*
> *They said, "We are afraid."*
> *"Come to the edge," He said.*
> *They came. He pushed them,*
> *And they flew.*[1]

To those who aspire to lead we issue a summons to move beyond the ordinary and into the realm of the extraordinary. In order to reach the highest level, one must seek and find a greater understanding about the essence of leadership—what it is and what it takes. One needs to constantly ask, "How am I doing?" In order to answer that question, it is important to have a framework with tangible indicators of progress. Such a guide elevates the consciousness of leadership and bridges the gap between coincidence and intentionality. This is the reason behind our use of a rubric.

A rubric is valuable as a vehicle to differentiate among levels of performance. However, the rubric alone is not powerful enough to constitute the true nucleus of our beliefs. We believe that this book's strongest value lies in the notion of "spirit movers." It is this unique component that separates this book from the myriads of others written to enlighten and encourage leaders. It is not uncommon for writers to describe leadership in terms of its essential components (facets). In addition, a portion of those writers further clarify their components by illustrating them at increments of proficiency (levels). However, the notion of identifying the inanimate forces (spirits) that are the fundamental prerequisites for ascendancy from one level to another (movers) is, to our knowledge, unique, catalytic, and worthwhile.

In some inventories, individuals are placed on a grid indicating what kind of leaders they are at a specific point in time and what their styles are as viewed both by themselves and others. The limitation of such vehicles is the absence of an authentic pathway affording upward movement on the grid. At best, inventories offer a "to do" list of actions, strategies, and behaviors. We believe that leadership is dynamic and not static. By drawing upon their spiritual strength, devoted leaders expand and improve their leadership capacity.

We think it may be useful at this time to expand on the terms "spirit" and "movers."

Spirit

Among the many definitions of the term *spirit*, the one that is most reflective of our intent comes from the Greek word *pnevma*, which means "the life force of a person." It might be helpful to view "spirit" as the energy that is the substantive, yet intangible, part of the essence of a person. It represents a vibrancy that permeates what has heart and meaning to a person.

The human spirit holds the promise for letting go of what does not work and for creating new solutions. The human spirit is both fragile and powerfully resilient. It is the source of insights, wisdom, and love. It is the centerpiece of any healthy organization. It is the least appreciated and yet the most critical source for productivity and creativity. The human spirit simply is. Dr. Margaret Hatcher has stated, "What has heart in our lives becomes the bridge to all we choose to be and do. Following the heart leads us to wholeness, to meaning."[2] The concept of spirit can also include will, enthusiasm, and strength. We expect that our words will be as useful as the desire and willingness of readers to apply their own life force to the theories we offer. The spirits of leaders are different from those of others in the broad, elemental belief that their actions will impact the behavior of those they lead and the character of the organization they serve. Without this belief, a person may have authority, yet never lead. Those with an expanded spirit, who commit their life force to leadership, are those who transform the world in which we all live. Without reservation we believe inspirational leaders are deeply cognizant of the character of their inner spirit and work to enhance the potential power of their life force for the enhancement of their mission and effectiveness.

Movers

Inherent in the word *movers* is motion. The possession of spirit, in and of itself, does not enable a person to lead. One often hears the saying, "The spirit is willing, but the flesh is weak."[3] In terms of ineffective leadership, the words might better be, "The spirit is willing but the motion is missing." Libraries are filled with volumes of the profound thinking of philosophers who observed and described the world but left the changing to others. For instance, Aristotle was a famous and brilliant philosopher with a powerful spirit, but his leadership was indirect. It was Alexander the Great, his most famous and important student, who was one of the most successful military commanders in history, and who was undefeated in battle. By the time of his death, he had conquered most of the world known to the ancient Greeks. Aristotle trained Alexander in rhetoric and literature and stimulated his interest in science, medicine, and philosophy. It was only when Alexander set into motion the spirit of Aristotle that the world was changed forever.

In today's world, we expect our leaders to combine their individual forces of spirit with the capacity for growth as leaders. They must not only be powerful in their essence, but they must also embrace the opportunity to expand their capacity to lead. What this really means is they must take action in order for the "spirit movers" of courage, love, optimism, humility, etc., to enable them to move from one level to the next. The important point to be made involves bringing consciousness to the potential for movement of the spirit to ascending levels. Inertia is neither acceptable nor viable in these times of rapid and dynamic change. This book is our attempt to offer both a pathway for the heart and the incentive to travel the journey it offers.

We recognize that our own journey in leadership is a story that continues to unfold. Within our roles and responsibilities, we aspire to model the highest levels of thinking and behaving we present in this book. It is our own guide to quality leadership, no matter the capacity in which we serve. In the spirit of invitation, we ask you to RSVP as follows.

RSVP

We invite you:

To make this book your own by adding that which has heart and meaning to you.

To remember that there are subtle measures of leadership that are not always quantitative.

To engage with others about the potential of the rubric and its usefulness.

To remember to articulate your life stories for the benefit of others.

To respond by offering us your best thinking after you've read our book.

To use the book as a tool in the development of others who aspire to lead.

To delve into the art of leadership, not just its science.

To humble yourself enough to be vulnerable to the ideas herein and confident enough to label some of them as "nonsense" in terms of your individual reality.

To examine the congruency between our concepts and the very nature of your essence (e.g., values, principles, beliefs).

Chapter 1

The Essence of a Leader

I n the chapters that follow, ten facets or elements that are paramount in the exercise of leadership are offered in the structure of a rubric along with the core element of "spirit movers" as discussed in the Invitation. An explanation of this structure is presented in detail in Chapter 2.

However, before proceeding to the rubric, we feel it is necessary for readers to be grounded in their uniqueness of spirit--the *essence* of who they are. This need to do so is based on the belief that who you are is what you will do. By beginning with thinking about and reflecting on their singular essence, readers will be prepared to personalize and authenticate the journey offered in the remainder of the book. This invites the question,

*"What is "essence" and what should leaders consider **prior** to positioning themselves on the rubric contained in this book?"*

Essence is primarily what constitutes the uniqueness and fundamental nature of a person. It represents what makes us who we are—what is intrinsic or inherent. Our essence is represented by our *values, beliefs, attitudes, principles, and inner spirit.*

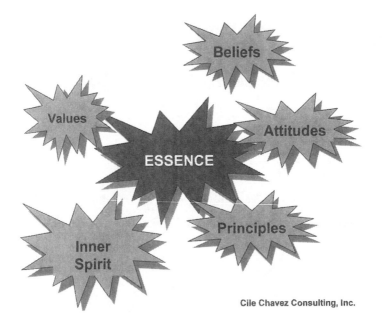

Cile Chavez Consulting, Inc.

These components can be considered the core of essence, and it is significant for leaders to reflect upon them and be able to articulate what they mean and how they are made manifest in their own lives. We have often heard the expression, "Who you are is what you will do." Essentially, our decisions, choices, actions, and behaviors mirror our essence even when we aren't fully aware. We express ourselves in multiple ways as a result of our values, beliefs, attitudes, principles, and inner spirit. Our essence can be viewed as a "container" within which our character as a leader will be defined by self and others. Unfortunately, in organizations leaders all too often hide their essence. They don't talk about it, honor it, or see the significance within it. This book facilitates a more conscious examination and discussion of one's essence in relation to organizational leadership.

We suggest ten primary facets of leadership constitute the curriculum of leadership. The way leaders live out these facets reflects their essence. The challenge for a leader is to know "self" in such a way as to continually grow intelligently, intentionally, and inspirationally as a human being.

So, what do we mean by values, beliefs, attitudes, principles, and inner spirit?

Values: As a noun, a value is that which has worth. In its verb form, to value means to think highly of or to prize. Our behaviors, however, often speak louder than words. It is questionable that people "value" something if it is not evident in the way they spend their resources (time, money, effort, etc). For instance, a leader might say, "I really believe in supporting my people." However, if there is little evidence of recognition of the achievements of those within the organization, the stated "value" is inauthentic, and the words become hollow to those deserving of the recognition and celebration.

Beliefs: Beliefs are what one accepts as being true. They can be judgments, a conviction, or in theology, faith. The following are examples of beliefs:

- Belief in the empowerment of others.
- Belief that organizations are living organisms.
- Belief that who you are is what you will do.
- Belief that all children can learn given appropriate time, resources, relevance, and encouragement.

Ultimately, one's beliefs help define one's essence and subsequently are reflected in one's behaviors.

Attitudes: We all can easily identify the attitude of another and generally categorize it as positive or negative. However, the term is broader than that. It is one's manner of acting, feeling, or thinking that shows one's disposition and opinions. Stephen Covey gives a helpful example when he speaks of people as having an attitude of abundance or scarcity. An example of scarcity might exist when formal power and influence is relegated to a few. An attitude of abundance would result in greater inclusion of people regardless of title or position.

Principles: The principles we hold to be true guide our lives and thus constitute our essence. Principles are typically a fundamental truth, doctrine, or motivating force. Examples are: fairness should guide our actions; honesty is the best policy; do unto others as you would have them do unto you; make decisions that are best for all concerned versus decisions of convenience.

Inner Spirit: Perhaps the hardest to define, this intangible energy is the underpinning of people's motivation and how they move in the world. In every person there is a uniqueness of spirit that makes him or her identifiable and separate from others. It is one's own truth.

All people have the previously stated components in their essence. *Each* individual's essence is made unique as a result of four key *influences*: the primary culture within which the person was brought up; life experiences; roles and responsibilities; and relationships.

It is not sufficient to simply articulate our values, beliefs, principles, attitudes, and spirit. Certainly, such an exercise helps leaders clarify who they are, thus enhancing their effectiveness through this awareness. Understanding the influences is equally critical in order to intelligently and thoughtfully alter thinking and subsequent behaviors to benefit self, others, and the organization.

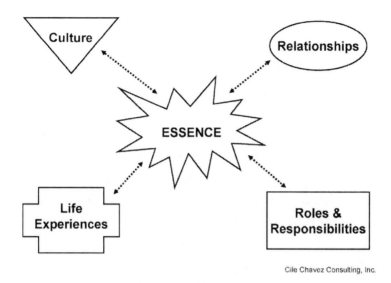

Cile Chavez Consulting, inc.

The Influence of *Culture:* The word "culture" has as its root the Latin word "colere," meaning "to cultivate." Generally, the word refers to the ability of humans to "cultivate" patterns of activity and the symbolic structures that give such activities significance and importance to a given group of people.

The Influence of *Life Experiences:* Experience refers to involvement in an activity or exposure to events or people over a period of time that leads to an increase in knowledge or skill.

The Influence of *Roles and Responsibilities:* Leaders are defined not just by the roles they have but also by their awareness of those they do not have and their consequent capacity to seek, find, and learn from those who "fill the gaps" in their experience.

The Influence of *Relationships:* Relationships refer to the intangible connections between two or more people or groups and their involvement with one another. Of most importance is the way they behave toward and feel about one another.

In this chapter we presented the concept of the "essence" of a leader and the critical importance of understanding the sources and influences of behaviors and actions. The intentional examination of a leader's essence can enhance his or her appreciation of why he or she functions at a particular level on the rubric. Also, for those who desire to progress to a higher level, we created the concept of "spirit movers," which serves as the energy source necessary to make such a movement possible. It is *critical* to note that if a leader's essence is not congruent with the spirit mover, the movement within the levels will be difficult and possibly not authentic.

For example, if there is a leader in your organization who, by his very nature, is limited in his ability to demonstrate inclusiveness, the quality of that person's efforts requiring teamwork will be inherently difficult. As a leader of leaders, you must continually ask yourself, "Who in this organization am I holding hostage for something he or she cannot be? What will I do about it?"

Another example is related to the importance of a leader being genuinely present with employees, as opposed to "phoning it in." A case in point is "Management by Wandering Around" (MBWA), which was coined and promoted as an important concept in management in the '80s. Leaders made every effort to be physically present throughout the organization. Some would, indeed, "wander around." Unfortunately, for those who adopted this practice because it was a prescription rather than part of their essence, the positive impact fell short of their intentions.

In summary, there is an important cause and effect relationship between the aforementioned external "influences" in one's life and the ultimate development of one's "core of essence." In order to achieve maximum benefit from the remainder of the book each reader is asked to reflect on his or her own uniqueness of spirit (what each brings to the table). Anchored by these reflections, the reader will be better prepared to navigate the rubric and ultimately transform his or her leadership.

RSVP
Given this discussion on essence, think of specific ways *your* essence has impacted the way you lead.

Quotation:
> *"The first responsibility of a leader is to define reality. The last is to say thank you. In between, the leader is a servant."*
> —*Max Depree, Author* [4]

Chapter 2

The Structure of the Rubric

E very book has bones (a conceptual skeleton) to which the writers add flesh (language) and through which they pump its marrow (concepts and context). In *The Spirit Movers: Attributes for Transforming Leadership,* we have chosen to use a rubric as the primary vehicle for communicating the facets we have found to constitute leadership. By describing ten chosen facets of leadership at rising levels of proficiency and significance, we have offered a specific and unique pathway for leaders to elevate themselves to inspired leadership. We have also endeavored to add value to the traditional rubric structure through the creation of the element we call "spirit movers." Just as language and concepts provide the "flesh" and "bones" of the book, so the spirit movers present its "heart."

What Is a Rubric?
A rubric is a framework that describes performance variables at several ascending levels of proficiency. It offers the user the capacity to examine his or her performance in relation to the levels.

Why Develop a Rubric?

- A rubric presents a visual, a portrait, and a framework for thinking. With one look, it allows the reader's eyes to move from the ordinary to the inspirational level.
- The rubric serves as a container capturing essential criteria for greatness and growth.
- A rubric has motion and fluidity and is not static. It has internal capacity for movement.
- A rubric is an effective tool for determining a level and quality of performance.
- A rubric allows the process of leadership development to be more objective and consistent.
- A rubric provides a format for accountability to established criteria.
- A rubric is a useful reflection and/or feedback tool regarding the effectiveness of the leader.

What Are the Specific Components of This Rubric?

This rubric is a framework that includes four key elements: facets, standards, level descriptions, and spirit movers. Additionally, scripts, indicators, quotes, questions, and elaborated rubrics enhance and expand the key elements. On the following pages, each of the components listed above is explained to greater depth.

Facets of Leadership: The facets are the "what" of leadership. Those chosen to be included in the book are: motivation, relationships, voice, vision, talent, change, time, decision making, health, and accountability.

- The facets offer an index of elements essential to leaders.
- They are vehicles for people to talk about leadership.

- They are a curriculum for the content of leadership.
- They answer the question, "What constitutes leadership?"

We acknowledge that other facets could be identified. Our hope is that the book will serve as a springboard for readers to identify additional facets constituting leadership within the context of their life experiences.

Standards: A standard expands the one-word facets to complete sentences describing what all leaders should know and be able to do. The standards for each of the ten facets follow.

Facet   Standard

Motivation: The leader knows and understands the intentions underlying his actions

Relationships: The leader is responsible for the character and quality of interactions between him and others in the organization.

Voice: The leader knows where, when, why, and how to express—both verbally and nonverbally—what matters to the organization.

Vision: The leader has the capacity to imagine a preferred future; articulate and clarify that image; and mobilize others toward making it a reality.

Talent: The leader refines and focuses his natural ability in order to capitalize on his gifts for a higher good.

Change: The leader orchestrates the organization's future direction and is persistent in staying the course.

Time: The leader uses both the quantity and quality of his time to advance the mission and vision of the organization.

Decision Making: The leader drives the actions of the organization by considering content, context, and processes.

Health: The leader establishes a state of personal and/or organizational well being in the physical, intellectual, and emotional dimensions.

Accountability: The leader accepts responsibility for personal and organizational results.

Level Descriptions: A typical rubric evaluating performance might use terms such as unsatisfactory, progressing, proficient, and advanced We find those terms inadequate when attempting to differentiate among the levels of a topic as complex as leadership. Rather, we believe describing three levels with the terms:Informed, Intentional, and Inspired will deepen one's reflection and judgment about the quality of leadership in self, others and organizations.

Level One: The Informed Level (Prepared Way)
Among the terms used to describe leaders at this level are: adequate, predictable, good, dependable, reactive, competent, and knowledgeable.

Level Two: The Intentional Level (Purposeful Way)
Among the terms used to describe leaders at this level are: conscious, deliberate, seeking greater understanding, reflective, learned, exercising judgment, and demonstrating integrated thinking.

Level Three: The Inspired Level (Passionate Way)
Among the terms used to describe leaders at this level are: compelling, enlightened, transformative, visionary, "shape shifter," exceptional, proactive, driven by possibilities, synergistic, and having greater depth.

Key Descriptors:

Key descriptors are given to each of the three levels for every facet. For example, in the Facet of Change, "Contentment" is used to describe the *Informed Level*; "Curiosity" represents the *Intentional Level*; and "Commitment" best captures the nature of the Inspired Level. Narratives are then provided to give context to the key words and assist the user in determining the proper placement on the rubric. The key word or words for each level of the facets are provided below. They are listed in the three columns to the right of the facets in the table.

Table 1:

Facets	Informed Level	Intentional Level	Inspired Level
Motivation	Rules and Regulations	Values and Principles	Covenants
Relationships	Independent	Collegial	Interdependent
Voice	Internal Dialogue	Communication	Deeper Conversation
Vision	Important	Significant	Historic
Talent	Developed	Dedicated	Endowed
Change	Contentment	Curiosity	Commitment
Time	Expeditious	Goal Setting	Soul Fulfilling
Decision Making	Isolated	Contextual	Wise
Health	Resilient	Proactive	Holistic
Accountability	Delegation	Ownership	Signature

It is important to note that there is a potential level we have chosen not to include. This is the level often described as unsatisfactory. Rather than spend time calling on negative energy to describe leadership that generates dissatisfaction, oppression, and an atmosphere of discontent or indifference, we chose to focus on traits and behaviors that affirm the positive possibilities of leadership.

In applying the rubric to ourselves and to other leaders, it became apparent that our rubric is not a static document. A leader is not guaranteed a permanent placement at a given level, having once performed at that level. For example, a move into a new organization might cause a leader who is normally courageous about change to be content for a while. During this time, that same leader might achieve the highest level of voice by having "deeper conversations" in an effort to understand the constitution and priorities of the organization. For this reason, the rubric will continue to serve the leader over time. Both in self-analysis and in analyzing the leadership of others, the movement within the rubric can be very enlightening.

Spirit Movers

In addition to standards, facets, and levels, this rubric also contains unique elements called "spirit movers." Spirit movers do not give a level its *identity*. Rather, they describe the specific attribute the leader must draw upon in order to ascend from one level to another. It is the spirit movers that give the rubric its life. Focus on a spirit mover enables and empowers leaders to elevate their performance with greater intention and effectiveness. Spirit movers answer the question, "What will it take?" While the standards, facets, and levels enable the readers to place themselves or others on the rubric based on current performance, the spirit movers are attributes holding hope for future repositioning and validate the work of those who have already become inspired leaders. Congruency between the spirit mover and one's essence cannot be emphasized enough.

Facet	Spirit Mover
Motivation	Trust
Relationships	Love
Voice	Presence
Vision	Courage
Talent	Passion
Change	Optimism
Time	Discernment
Decision Making	Humility
Health	Balance
Accountability	Truth

Scripts

In each chapter, scripts are offered that illustrate the kinds of comments a leader might make at a specific level. For instance, in the facet of accountability, delegation is the criteria for placement at the *informed level*. Thus a leader might say, "This is a task I don't want my fingerprints on. I think it's a job for a task force." In this statement, it is obvious that the leader is transferring the responsibility and accountability to someone else.

Indicators

Each chapter includes examples of behaviors indicating the specific level at which the leader is functioning. For example, in the facet of voice, at the *intentional level* (communication), an indicator is: "Leaders make a conscious effort to include appropriate persons in the feedback process."

RSVPs

At the end of every facet, we have offered an RSVP, which serves as a call to action. Each RSVP challenges readers to "go deeper"

in order to expand and apply the facet within the context of
their experience.

Quotations

We have chosen to honor the thinking of others by including
relevant quotations in each facet.

Elaborated Rubrics

An elaborated rubric can be found at the end of each chapter. This
rubric will include standards, levels, criteria, and organizational
indicators. Criteria that are common threads within the facet are
differentiated by level. Organizational indicators cite possible
manifestations at the organizational level. The elaborated rubrics,
when combined with the general rubric at the end of this chapter,
offer a synopsis of the key components of the book. They are
provided for the purposes of review, discussion, and reflection.

The Rubric

On the following page, the reader will find the complete rubric
with the Spirit Movers noted below each facet. It is the cornerstone
document in which the soul of our book resides.

A Rubric for Transforming Leadership

FACET	Informed (Prepared Way)	Intentional (Purposeful Way)	Inspired (Passionate Way)
Motivation Trust	Rules, Regulations	Values/ Principles	Covenants
Relationships Love	Independent	Collegial	Interdependent
Voice Presence	Internal Dialogue	Communication	Deeper Conversation
Vision Courage	Important	Significant	Historic
Talent Passion	Developed	Dedicated	Endowed
Change Optimism	Contentment	Curiosity	Commitment
Time Discernment	Expeditious	Goal Setting	Soul Fulfilling
Decision-making Humility	Isolated	Contextual	Wise
Health Balance	Resilient	Proactive	Holistic
Accountability Truth	Delegation	Ownership	Signature

Chapter 3

The Facet of Motivation

*"The greater the loyalty of a group toward the group, the
greater is the motivation among the members to achieve the
goals of the group, and the greater the probability that the
group will achieve its goals."*[5]
—Rensis Likert, Organizational Psychologist

*S*tandard: **The leader knows and understands the
intentions underlying his actions**

We often ask the question, "What is your motivation?"
Essentially, we want to know the reason *why* someone does or
does not act in a certain way. The driving force for functioning
within an organization may vary depending on the leader's
internal motivation. Sometimes we may be guided by rules and
regulations, values and principles, or a covenant. We consider
these as three levels or stages from which leaders guide their
organizations. Each level provides a core basis or inner drive
for doing something or for acting in a certain way. Most people
who work within an organization quickly come to understand

the driving forces for "how things are done around here." Organizational motivation is often expressed in the mission statement. However, it is critical that the mission statement be both current and prominent if it is to add value.

Informed Level: Rules and Regulations

Whenever we enter an organization, a culture, a school, or a district, we assume there are established rules and regulations. We quickly come to sense there are specific norms, expectations, and boundaries for behaviors. These are intended to keep order and to guide people into certain ways of thinking and behaving. Some examples might include: strict adherence to schedules; practices and/ or procedures for connecting with people in different departments; and formalities for communications. Typically, we seek to know and understand, and comply with the rules and regulations because our worldview might tell us this is how to succeed.

Informed leadership in relation to motivation can be characterized as leadership that recognizes the merits of rules and regulations and indeed, may author the rules and regulations. They come to know that "good" leaders are recognized and rewarded for living out the rules on a consistent basis.

At this level, predictability, common expectations, compliance and a certain degree of uniformity in behaviors are held to be important. However, leaders at this level might call into question and attempt to change some rules and regulations based upon their desire for efficiency and effectiveness.

Scripts

"That's the way we do things around here."

"It's for the good of the order."

"Let's get out the policy book and see what it says about this issue."

"There it is in black and white."

Indicators

- There are relatively low numbers of risk-taking behaviors.
- There is an attitude of fitting in before you can stand out.
- The policy book might be extensive and referenced frequently.
- Risk-takers will be frustrated.

Intentional Level: Values and Principles

When organizations articulate their values, they typically display them in visible places for the employees and community. Essentially, they are communicating what is important to them, what they hold to be significant, what matters the most. It is assumed that at some point in time these values and principles were developed through a collaborative process with the intention of communicating how people will "be" in the workplace and what others can expect of them. Enunciating critical values requires a commitment to action equal to the proclamations.

Leaders who function at this level desire behaviors that are value-based, not just rule-based. They essentially want to uplift the human spirit and develop the character within the organization. They believe that the potential for improvement resides within individuals. The organization is a place that fosters human growth and potential. To this end, the development of principles serves as a guide to the fulfillment of the values.

Scripts

"I wonder if our various employee groups could support this action."

"Is that behavior consistent with who we are?"

"This isn't about rules; it's about what is right."

"It's okay if someone else takes the lead on this."

Indicators

- Familiarizing new employees with the principles/values of the organization is an essential part of the induction process.
- Value statements, such as codes of ethics or operating principals are prominently displayed and are frequently referenced.
- One aspect of accountability is the adherence to the accepted values.
- Rewards and recognition are used to honor those who live out the values.
- People serve as the conscience of their own organization.

Inspired Level: Covenant

When people within an organization behave at the covenant level, their commitments to one another are almost sacred; they literally promise to behave in agreed upon ways. The ways reflect an alignment between the very personal values of the individual, group values, and the mission of the organization. Evidence of the covenant is in the passion for the work and the joy in living it out. There is a drive to fulfill a shared vision of working together that is extraordinary. The covenant provides both reason and energy for transcending those forces that typically keep people and organizations at an ordinary level. A covenantal relationship fills deep needs, and thus people can deal more effectively with conflict and change. All too often, relationships are contractual in nature. They are based on formal agreements and reciprocity.

Leaders must invest in covenant relationships for the highest good to be achieved.

Covenants do not come easily because they require accountability for one's intentions and in fact, one's very essence. They are not only what you do but also who you are. As such, they transcend common forms of "evaluation" of performance. The work becomes the landscape for becoming the best self. This means that there is great openness and vulnerability in communications and action. The highest value is to serve one another for individual actualization and for the greater good.

Scripts

"This isn't just my job; it's my passion."

"Tell me what you really think and feel."

"Whatever it takes!"

"I may not be able to express it, but I feel a deep understanding of the need."

Indicators

- People with a covenant are not influenced by gossip or petty behaviors of others.
- The covenant is so internalized that they do not require reference.
- Communications stay focused on deeper and more meaningful discussions.
- When a person minimizes, negates, or questions the value of the covenant, he or she is encouraged, if not directed, to realize he or she has a choice.
- People assume best intentions.

In this chapter we offered three levels in the Facet of Motivation: rules and regulations; values and principles; and covenant. To summarize from a developmental perspective, clarity can easily be determined when the driving motivation is that of rules and regulations. Doing business is simply following the rules. However, when the leader intentionally invites a dialogue on what is valued and the principles that will protect those values, the motivation for behaviors becomes more complex and holds greater meaning for people. As one continues the journey to greatness in the *inspired level* of leadership, symbols become more significant and the spirit of the organization is centered on empowerment and transformation. In essence, relationships are covenantal when they motivate, inspire, and align the goals of individuals and groups toward a common future.

Spirit Mover: Trust

Trust is the currency for the development of covenants. Trust is not a commodity that can be obtained with favoritism, mandates, or intimidation. There is no inherent value in the statement, "You should trust me." Rather, trust is earned through experiences, great and small.

It is reasonable to state that leaders desire to be trusted by their colleagues, associates, and employees at all levels within the organization. The same is true for the employees; they want to be trusted by those in leadership positions as well as by their colleagues.

Therefore, if a leader wants to move from the *informed level* to the intentional or *inspired levels* in terms of motivation, the leader has to examine his motives for focusing so strongly on compliance with rules and regulations. The power of leading with values, principles, and a covenant is the assurance that greater trust will exist throughout the organization.

Alan Axelrod, in his book, *When the Buck Stops with You: Harry S. Truman on Leadership*, stated, "Trust is among a leader's most valued treasures. You need both to receive and to give trust; and when you give it, do so with scrupulous discrimination and boundless generosity—a difficult combination."[6]

The concept of trust is used frequently, and yet, its meaning and what it looks like in an organization, a family, or a friendship is not always well articulated. What does constitute trust? We believe there are core elements in the spirit of trust, and we present them using the letters within the word:

T = *Tell the Truth*

Truth telling can mean sharing the reality of circumstances; giving honest, yet kind, feedback; validating with specificity; and taking responsibility for decisions and actions.

R = *Respond Consistently*

Typically trust is built by exhibiting, with integrity, a consistent, predictable response to events and circumstances. The benefit is greater emotional security. This, of course, is easiest when values and guiding principles are clear and universally accepted.

U = *Understand Others*

We ask readers to think of those they truly trust. To what degree is that trust built upon the confidence you have that others have demonstrated a genuine interest in your point of view? This confidence is in direct correlation to the level of trust we give and receive. Additionally, appreciating another's situation, challenges, and desires results in trust building.

S = *Seek the Higher Ground*

When a person behaves in a manner that honors self and others rather than "shrinking" or demeaning others, trust is built. There may be good reason to "scratch with the chickens," but it takes character and commitment to excellence to "soar with the eagles" and thus seek the higher ground in human behavior.

T = *Take Action*

"Walk your talk" is a phrase that has a common interpretation. Typically it means people follow through on promises, engage in constructive problem solving, and create opportunities out of challenges.

If the above behaviors are a reflection of one's motivation in all interactions with others, trust will surely follow.

We all aspire to be deemed, both personally and professionally, as trustworthy. However, the path to trustworthiness is marked with both internal and external obstacles. Among the barriers that might be faced are: fear, safety, losses, and perceived consequences. Regardless of challenges and obstacles, the highest value is to continue the journey to trustworthiness.

The power and significance of trust is well framed by Dr. Margaret Hatcher in her field book, *The Teacher Archetype:* "Without the quality of trust, there can be no healing of the workplace, no depth of communication of vision and meaning, no community effort for manifesting the vision, and no buy-in and support of the leadership of the organization. Like authenticity and integrity, trust is the glue that creates shared meaning and purpose, integration, connection and community in an organization. In fact, trust is possibly the most powerful motivator for excellence and high performance in the workplace."[7]

With respect to a leader's behavior, Kouzes and Posner state, "If leaders want higher levels of performance that come with trust and collaboration, they must demonstrate trust *in* others before asking for trust *from* others."[8]

We all know the importance of trust, yet we don't talk about it in a manner that honors the reality and degree of its existence. Leaders have to have the courage to call for the question, *"What have we informally agreed to never talk about?"* If a leader can have an agenda with this one question, all participants will be free to speak openly and come close to understanding what living in a covenant looks like. And subsequently, there will be fewer clandestine parking lot conversations.

RSVP

List three steps you could take *today* to create a more trustworthy environment.

Quotation:

> *"Trust men and they will be true to you; treat them greatly and they will show themselves great."*[9]
> —Ralph Waldo Emerson

Spirit Movers: Attributes for Transforming Leadership

Elaborated Rubric for the Facet of Motivation

Facet	Informed (Prepared Way)	Intentional (Purposeful Way)	Inspired (Passionate Way)
Motivation	**Rules, Regulations**	**Values/Principles**	**Covenants**
The reason leaders do what they do – the basis for their behavior.	Leaders recognize the need for rules and regulations. At times they author the rules. Rewards are based upon living out the rules.	Values and principles are the basis for leaders' behaviors. They inspire character development in the organization.	Leaders create a covenant with others in the organization. A shared vision and passion for the work is the basis for behavior. People work together for the greater good.
The Spirit Mover Is *Trust*	**Organizational Indicators:**	**Organizational Indicators:**	**Organizational Indicators:**
	• Little risk taking. • Policy book frequently referenced. • Need to fit in. • Uniformity in behaviors	• Values predominately displayed. • Accountability and rewards based adhering to the values • Organizational conscience resides in people.	• The covenant is internalized to a high degree. • People hold positive assumptions about behavior. • Leaders trust and are trusted.

Chapter 4

The Facet of Relationships

*"The great leaders are like the best conductors—they reach
beyond the notes to reach the magic in the players."*[10]
—Blaine Lee, Author & Consultant

Standard: **The leader is responsible for the character and
quality of interactions between himself and others in
the organization.**

The quotation above speaks to the power and promise of
quality relationships based on a leader's deep understanding of
the gifts and talents of others. In leadership, as in life, we are not
separate; we must reach the magic of all that is possible through
building and nurturing relationships.

Why are relationships so critical to the success of organizations?
Why must leaders invest heavily in creating and fostering positive
relationships? And do relationships have equal value to defined
roles and responsibilities? One cannot lead in a vacuum. One can
possess a compelling mission, sterling strategies, and a brilliant
action plan, but none of those matters if there are not *people*

with and for whom one leads. People make things happen. People bring life to visions, missions, and purposes. Investment in relationships is an investment in the achievement of goals.

At its nucleus, leadership is about developing a caring environment that elevates the human spirit and enables everyone in the organization to feel the importance of their contributions, both individually and collectively. Some of the leavening agents that make such elevation possible are empathy, trust, honesty, and optimism. But what is the source of these attributes? How can we examine our lives to even understand and subsequently breathe life into the kind of relationships we want? How can we intelligently guide our actions within the context of relationship to the benefit of ourselves and others?

Whenever leaders enter an organization, they bring their essence and all that it constitutes with them. They subsequently influence and help shape the organization through their relationships with others. And it is critical to note that this is not a one-way process; the culture of the organization can also impact the leader. Clearly, it is through relationships that the journey to the fulfillment of vision and mission is accomplished.

The rubric for the facet of relationships recognizes three levels: independent, collegial, and interdependent. The essence of a leader is revealed within these levels, and thus, it is significant for leaders to know and understand what it means to function at each level. The promise and consequences are unique to each level of relationships.

Perhaps the most important and challenging relationship any of us has is with ourselves. How we are within serves as an indicator as to the type and quality of relationships we have with others in our personal and professional lives.

Informed Level: Independent

When leaders function at the level of independence, it may be due to the uniqueness of their role and responsibilities and expectations with regard to accountability. This isn't an indictment of character but rather a situation of need and circumstance. Sometimes a leader just needs to function independently. Leaders who must advise a governing board of personnel issues or offer a judgment of consequence of board decisions may behave in an independent manner, given the context. To stay at this level in all endeavors, however, will result in isolation, loss of trust and transparency, and limited opportunities to persuade and influence people throughout the organization.

Using sports as an example, a professional golfer such as Anika Sorenstam is independent when she is on the course. Her individual performance is the sole determinant of her success. However, as a member of the Solheim Cup team, Sorenstam's performance is one of collaboration and team success, which would move her to the *intentional level* of relationship.

Scripts

"I would rather do it myself."

"Collaboration is a waste of time; we all know the needed outcome."

"I'm sorry, but I'm really not in a position to discuss that issue with you."

Indicators

- Independent, relentless practice in a skill or talent is evident.
- Leaders keep their own counsel.
- Relating with others may be coincidental rather than purposeful.
- The feelings and experiences of others are acknowledged.

Intentional Level: Collegial

When relationships are positive, constructive, and mutually respectful, the opportunity for growth and development is enhanced. Collegial leaders understand and foster the concept of synergy. Stephen Covey elaborated on the concept of synergy when he stated, "If you are in an arena that requires teamwork, do everything you can to get rid of competition and to get to synergy; reward people for cooperating, for teamwork, and for giving their best ideas."[11] When synergy is evident, not only is productivity high but the relationships are also characterized as having a high level of generosity and integrity.

Leaders who understand and function well at this level listen and engage because they see the advantage of doing so. It is a value to represent others, and therefore input, collaboration, and dialogue are critical. At this stage, one can be true to self and not have to agree with others to be effective. As a colleague of others, one values a minority view or opinion. One acknowledges differences.

Scripts

"We can't proceed without others' input."

"This is a team effort."

"My colleagues and I don't have to agree on this, but we respect each other's opinion."

"Our success depends on each of us showing up."

Indicators

- Interest in each other's work is evident and individual successes are celebrated..
- Regardless of differences in points of view, respect for the individual is a constant.

- There is evidence of playfulness and lightheartedness.
- Creativity is easy, and there are few guarded behaviors.
- These leaders are sympathetic.

Inspired Level: Interdependent

Caring as a prerequisite for effective leadership is often expressed in the phrase: Nobody cares how much you know, until they know how much you care. In the inspired category, leaders not only foster and nurture positive relationships, but they also understand and embrace the knowledge that those relationships are more than an end in themselves. Clearly, relationships have a direct impact on the success of the organization, in reaching its goals, and in achieving its mission.

At the highest level of the facet of relationships, leaders understand one fundamental truth. They recognize that every time they are in the presence of one or more individuals, they have the opportunity to develop relationships that elevate the human spirit. Among the behaviors that characterize leaders at this level are:

- They *honor and value* others' presence, experiences, stories, and truths.
- They *behave* in an inclusive and fair-minded way.
- They *demonstrate* that they care how their attitudes, decisions, and actions will affect others.
- They *seek* out the perceptions, opinions, and ideas of others regardless of title and role.
- They *establish* a reputation of being trustworthy, honest, optimistic, and fair.
- They *listen* more than they talk.

Not only are their lives and the lives of others enriched by the relationships they share, but when human spirits are elevated in the workplace, the work to which they are dedicated also achieves a higher plane. By relying on mutual assistance, support, cooperation, and relationships among all members and constituents, a work force is able to realize true interdependence.

During World War II, Franklin Roosevelt observed, "We now realize, as we have never before, our interdependence on each other—that we cannot merely take, but we must be willing to sacrifice for the good of a common discipline, because, without such discipline, no progress is made, no leadership becomes effective."[12] The power of interdependence, though more obvious in a national crisis situation, can be equally as powerful or more powerful in an environment where an atmosphere of peace and an opportunity for reflection prevail. When the same intense, collaborative energy is applied to "board rooms" that is applied to "war rooms," the potential for greatness is present in an organization.

Scripts
"I feel like I'm a member of Cirque Du Soleil."

"Remember the time when we …"

"We will create something that could not humanly exist without the contributions of each of us."

"When I work with this team, I feel most synergistic."

"Congratulations! This calls for a celebration."

Indicators
- These leaders are empathetic.
- There are ample personal and organizational stories and the freedom to share them.

- Laughter and fun are evident.
- Leaders share the success in all aspects of the organization.
- The work of others is not seen in isolation, but as a part of the whole.

Spirit Mover: Love

We thought for a long time about what really constitutes the spirit mover or energy necessary for the *Facet of Relationships* and could only conclude ... *love*.

It is the power of loving that we know expands our capacity for authentic relationships with ourselves and others. The love we speak of in this context is love of humanity—our deep connection as human beings.

Clearly, the spirit mover of love is about abundance of human spirit. Love means giving: giving of time, compassion, and empathy. Not only is love about *giving*, but it is also about *forgiving*. Forgiveness is an expression of love. An organization can't forgive its people, but the people within it can forgive each other. If you want to work in an environment of collegiality or interdependence, forgiveness is integral.

Quotations about love have been a matter of record as long as people have attempted to capture their feelings with words. Because love has such incredible breadth (e.g., love of country, people, pets, sports, etc.), it is important that we frame love within the context of this book. Tina Turner sings, "What's love got to do with it?" Our answer to Tina is, "When it comes to leadership, love has *everything* to do with it." Leadership without love is like a body without a heart. It has no pulse, no core, and no life. To assist us in our definition, we have chosen the words of others about the phenomenon called "love" and we have interpreted and applied their thoughts to the subject of leadership.

1. *"Being deeply loved by someone gives you strength while loving someone deeply gives you courage."*[13]
    —Lao Tzu

To leaders this means …

Genuine, mutual caring adds power and dimension to the work at hand. Unhampered by uncertainty in relationships, both the leader and those being served are free to bring valor to their mission.

2. *"Love takes off masks that we fear we cannot live without and know we cannot live within."*[14]
    —James Baldwin

To leaders this means …

Those leaders who have confidence in their relationships present themselves without needing to hide behind a façade. Their honesty engenders the same level of candor in others.

3. *"It is only with the heart that one can see rightly; what is essential is invisible to the eye."*[15]
    —Antoine De Saint Exupery

To leaders this means…

Data analysis, observed behaviors, and written communications, while important, are insufficient means to access the very deepest truths. Only with the "insight" of intuition can feelings for which there are no words, graphs, or e-mails be illuminated. A wise leader has a 20/20 heart.

4. *"In order to create, there must be a dynamic force, and what force is more potent than love?"*[16]
—Igor Stravinsky

To leaders this means ...

Maximum creativity is available to those who use the power of love as the Spirit Mover or "dynamic force" in their relationships. The degree to which they are capable of giving and receiving love will have a direct bearing on their capacity to achieve interdependence.

5. *"If you love someone, let them go, for if they return, they were always yours. And if they don't, they never were."*[17]
—Kahlil Gibran

To leaders this means ...

It is impossible to control the minds and hearts of others. At most, a domineering leader may be able to silence those with whom he or she works. But is a mistake to interpret silence as consent or agreement.

6. *"You, yourself, as much as anybody in the entire universe, deserve your love and affection."*[18]
—Buddha

To leaders this means ...

Those who denigrate themselves are necessarily preoccupied with their own inner healing. Only when they are able to resolve their own issues are they free to create loving relationships with others.

7.   *"Love is the force that ignites the spirit and binds teams together."*[19]

    —Phil Jackson, NBA Coach

To leaders this means …

Without love, the "ignition" of spirit cannot take place and the "binding" of the team is vulnerable. When love is present, good chemistry is evident.

8.   *"Love cures people—both the ones who give it and the ones who receive it."*[20]

    —Dr. Karl Menninger, Founder of the Menninger Clinic

To leaders this means…

Loving organizations are healthy organizations.

9.   *"We look forward to the time when the power to love will replace the love of power. Then will our world know the blessings of peace."*[21]

    —William Gladstone, nineteenth-century British Prime Minister

To leaders this means …

In an organization where the leader loves power more than people, peace is not achievable. People have an intuitive resistance to dominance that will certainly arise in such conditions, bringing conflict, either overt or covert, with it.

10. *"It is not how much you do but how much love you put into the doing and sharing with others that is important. Try not to judge people. If you judge others then you are not giving love.".*[22]
—Mother Theresa

To leaders this means ...

Inherent in this quote is an apparent dilemma for leaders. How can a leader perform the task of supervision/evaluation without judging? In a loving organization the supervisor and employees form trusting partnerships in which the focus is on self-improvement rather than top-down judgment.

RSVP

Given your current position, who is the greatest impediment to the *inspired level* of Interdependence? Reach out to that person right away to forge a new alliance or lovingly help him or her find a better career match—even if *you* are that person.

Quotation:

"Love and compassion are necessities, not luxuries. Without them humanity cannot survive."[23]
—Dalai Lama

Spirit Movers: Attributes for Transforming Leadership

Elaborated Rubric for the Facet of Relationships

FACET	Informed (Prepared Way)	Intentional (Purposeful Way)	Inspired (Passionate Way)
Relationships	**Independent**	**Collegial**	**Interdependent**
Standard: *The leader is responsible for the character and quality of interactions between him and others in the organization.*	Leader functions independently due to style, unique role, and/or responsibilities.	Leader creates collaborative synergy leading to better solutions than could be produced independently. Leader understands the value of collaboration, input, and dialogue.	Leader understands that relationships have direct impact on the organization and its success. She honors and values others' experiences, stories, and truths. She views each interaction as an opportunity to elevate the human spirit.
The Spirit Mover Is *Love.*	**Organizational Indicators:** • Relating to others may be coincidental. • Leaders keep their own counsel. • Limited collaboration.	**Organizational Indicators:** • Expressed interest in each other's work • Creativity encouraged • People open, not guarded. • Minority views or opinions valued	**Organizational Indicators:** • Success has its genesis in human relationships. • Personal and organizational stories are frequently shared. • Work of others is seen as part of the whole. • Laughter and lightheartedness are evident.

Chapter 5

The Facet of Voice

"The human voice can never reach the distance that is covered by the still, small voice of conscience".[24]
—Mohandas Mahatma Gandhi

Standard: **The leader knows where, when, why, and how to express, both verbally and nonverbally, what matters to the organization.**

This facet addresses voice as a concept, not just a process of using one's vocal cords. The voice of a leader extends well beyond the spoken word and encompasses all forms of communication and expression. Dimensions of voice include not only how leaders express themselves but also where, when, and for what purpose their voices are used or not used. For example, no voice has been louder than the unspoken voice of Rosa Parks when she refused to move on the bus.

Voice also includes the ability to listen, reflect, and expand one's capacity for voice based on the wisdom of others. Unrest in an organization is often captured in the expression, "My voice was never heard." Rather than their spoken words, people who say this are usually referring to the fact that their opinions—verbal, nonverbal, or written—were never considered. Conversely, in higher functioning organizations, people feel they have been listened to, even if they do not agree with the decision. This keeps the vision vivid.

The leader's voice is both the most powerful and the most scrutinized vehicle at his or her disposal in the leadership process. Indeed, it has been said, "If you change your words, you may change the world." It is essential that your voice be used thoughtfully, purposefully, and compassionately. In order to maximize the effectiveness of voice a leader must be fully present, available, and without preconceived outcomes.

Informed Level: Internal Dialogue

At times, leaders prefer to keep their own counsel. Reasons may include failure to trust, inability to express oneself, arrogance, shyness, and/or lack of confidence. Confining one's voice to "internal dialogue" ultimately limits the knowledge the leader holds inside and eliminates the benefit of others' thinking. Regardless of the depth of personal knowledge possessed, leaders who do not acknowledge the voices of others may be seen as arbitrary or narrow minded. Whether or not the people in the organization challenge the wisdom of the decisions resulting from a leader's internal dialogue, they do not feel professionally valued as a result of their exclusion from the process. "I" statements dominate communications.

We must acknowledge that there are occasions when, restricted by time or circumstance, a leader has no choice other than to rely upon his empirical knowledge. However, when isolated thinking is a consistent preference rather than an occasional necessity, it limits the potential impact of the leader's voice.

Scripts

"In my considered opinion, we should do. ..."

"I'd tell her/him what I think, but would it matter?"

"Where'd that idea come from?"

"Do we have to have a committee for everything?"

Indicators

- More value is put on compliance after the fact than on input prior to a decision.
- There is limited sharing of ideas.
- Decision-making is efficient though not necessarily effective.

Intentional Level: Communication

By definition, communication is the exchange of information between individuals by means of speaking, writing, or using a common system of signs or behaviors. It is distinct from the *informed level* of internal dialogue by virtue of the word "exchange." At this level, the leader's ability to listen comes into play along with a sincere desire to afford others the opportunity for input into the decisions and direction of the organization. Thus the leader's voice is viewed as more reflective of broader thinking than in isolation. At this level, virtually any topic, from insignificant to critical, can be the focus of the communication. What separates the *intentional level* from the *inspired level* is the depth and nature of the exchanges.

Enlightened leaders know that their individual contributions of insights, ideas, and strategies, offered in a formative manner, are critical to the overall quality of the work. Leaders do not withhold their voice. They are not timid about offering their empirical wisdom, based on experience,

Scripts:

> "Please sign up to be on a committee. Your input is valuable."
>
> "Our document will reflect many sources of input."
>
> "My door is always open."
>
> "I pride myself on answering all e-mails quickly."

Indicators

- There is positive acceptance of people toward the leader's speeches and written communications because a sense of presence has been previously established.
- Leaders make a conscious effort to include appropriate persons in the communications process.
- Efforts are made to reach out through telecommunications/technology.

Inspired Level: Deeper Conversation

Robert Louis Stevenson said, "All speech, written or spoken, is a dead language, until it finds a willing and prepared hearer."[25] A leader's voice is most effective when the conditions have been set to afford all parties the opportunity to be heard and to arrive at a collective wisdom which exceeds the capacity of any one individual. "Deeper conversations" occur when ego is left at the door and openness, empathy, sincerity, and thoughtfulness fill the room. Dr. Stephanie Marshall in her book, *The Power to Transform,* describes deeper conversations as ones "imbued with mindful intent ... these conversations are about deep learning, deep questions, deep knowledge generation and deep wisdom creation."[26] The focus is on creating meaning and purpose. The results of such conversations, when expressed clearly by the leader, have the potential to move organizations confidently to a preferred future. They minimize the time spent "selling" an idea, because employees are confident that the decisions are reflective of more than just the thinking of the leader.

This level is distinguished from the *intentional level* of communications by the depth of the conversations that occur and the profundity of the topics. Deeper conversations recognize and bring into play a universal consciousness that connects to those not in the room. Participants say the dialogue has heart and meaning. Additionally, these deeper conversations are not hurried and honor equality in perspectives. The leaders show their commitment with their time, energy and physical presence. The role of a leader in a deeper conversation cannot be delegated. The nature of communication with an inspired leader is elevated and contains discussions of significance to the organization and those it serves. Thus, when the leader's voice is used, it is heeded as an extension of the voices of those within the group at large.

For some, the term, "deeper conversation" may conjure up images of well-planned, one-on-one, private dialogues. Though such settings may be productive, the realities of time and circumstance do not always make them possible. There are occasions when critical exchanges must occur at once, with no opportunity for preparation. At the *inspired level*, leaders have the capacity to engage in deeper conversations, regardless of the environmental variables. As Goethe said, "Talent develops in quiet places, character in the full current of human life."[27] The Facet of Voice at its highest level involves unguarded courage and genuine, personal vulnerability regarding the most deeply seated issues and feelings.

Below, we offer some examples of questions that hold the promise of deeper conversations.

1. Of all the things we could do, what must we do?
2. Are we spending our time, talent, and resources on those things we hold paramount in the spirit of our work?
3. How do we come to know what has heart and meaning to those we serve?
4. What does "being present" look like?
5. What are some assumptions we have made about our work that no longer will serve us?

Scripts

"I wouldn't miss one of these meetings for anything."

"We feel so energized by our last interaction."

"We love it that we don't waste a lot of our time on trivial pursuits."

Indicators

- There is enthusiastic anticipation of the leader's speeches and written communications.
- Meetings are thoughtful and of substance, avoiding minutia.
- There is recurring clarity of purpose, mission, and vision. There are opportunities for people to genuinely share their fears, hopes, and what stands in the way.
- Example of a deeper conversation: "We hold these truths to be self evident …" (the crafting of the Declaration of Independence).

Spirit Mover: Presence

The spirit of presence is an energy that brings an unspoken rapport between and among people. It encompasses a sense of caring, vulnerability, and curiosity and a commitment of self.

Presence is a way of being so completely integrated into a time and space with others that the high value of the interactions is clear. Intentional leaders make a genuine effort to reach out, communicate, and involve others. An inspired leader holds the space, with his or her very presence, for a deeper conversation. For leaders who desire to have a profound impact, the investment of their voice is essential.

One is reminded of two cars heading down the same road parallel to each other. They attempt to communicate through open windows while still moving. While this can be done, it is not an easy feat. The drivers must focus on the highway and the conversation simultaneously. If either car is ahead or behind, the voices are lost to each other.

Maintaining one's presence is similarly difficult. On some occasions, the leader may anticipate what the other person is about to say and jump in to move the topic forward. However accurate such an assumption may be about *content*, to preempt it from unfolding naturally negates the opportunity to both hear and feel the *context* of the words from the speaker's perspective. Also, hastening the process may feel patronizing or dismissive.

Slowing the conversation down because of distractions or inattention may also have negative consequences. The ability to focus on the vision of the future, while sustaining a sincere, active voice in the present, is an artful skill that is the underpinning of a deeper conversation.

It is critical to understand that presence does not mean the leader's voice is paramount. For followers to believe the leader is truly present with them may mean the leader never says a word. Leaders hear the unspoken questions and respond by pressing for deeper conversations. It is through active listening, body language, and attention to setting that the leader can demonstrate true presence.

RSVP

Find a person with whom you really need or want to have a "deeper conversation" and schedule that meeting without delay.

Quotation:

> *"When you surrender to what is and so become fully present, the past ceases to have any power. You do not need it anymore. Presence is the key. Now is the key."*[28]
> —Eckhart, Tolle, *The Power of Now*

Spirit Movers: Attributes for Transforming Leadership

Elaborated Rubric for the Facet of Voice

FACET	Informed (Prepared Way)	Intentional (Purposeful Way)	Inspired (Passionate Way)
Voice	Internal Dialogue	Communication	Deeper Conversation
Standard: *The leader knows where, when, why, and how to express, both verbally and nonverbally, what matters to the organization.*	The leader chooses to keep her own counsel. The leader typically does not seek or acknowledge the voices of others.	The depth and nature of exchanges informs decisions and actions of the leader.	Voice is reflective of the depth of conversations and profoundness of topics which are encouraged and inspired by the leader.
The Spirit Mover Is Presence.	**Organizational Indicators:** <ul><li>Compliance is highly valued</li><li>Decision making is efficient, though not necessarily effective.</li><li>Sharing of ideas is limited.</li></ul>	**Organizational Indicators:** <ul><li>Committee work is valued.</li><li>Right people, right work, right place, right time.</li><li>Multiple kinds of media are valued and used.</li></ul>	**Organizational Indicators:** <ul><li>People care more about quality of time than quantity of time.</li><li>Clarity of purpose, mission, and vision are evident.</li><li>Collective wisdom is noted and celebrated at a conscious level.</li></ul>

Chapter 6

The Facet of Vision

*"The very essence of leadership is (that) you have a vision.
It's got to be a vision you articulate clearly and forcefully on
every occasion. You can't blow and uncertain trumpet."*[29]
—Rev. Theodore Hesburgh, President Emeritus,
University of Notre Dame

***S**tandard:* **The leader has the capacity to imagine a preferred future; articulate and clarify that image; and mobilize others toward making it a reality.**

In virtually every book or article on leadership, "vision" is deemed a cornerstone of one's successful leadership. Robert F. Kennedy perhaps captured the significance and power of vision when he said:

Some believe there is nothing one man or one woman can do against the enormous array of the world's ills—against misery, against ignorance, or injustice and violence. Yet many of the world's great movements, of thought and action, have flowed from the work of a single man. A young monk began the Protestant reformation, a young general extended an empire from Macedonia to the borders of the earth, and a young woman reclaimed the territory of France. It was a young Italian explorer who discovered the New World, and 32 year old Thomas Jefferson who proclaimed that all men are created equal. "Give me a place to stand," said Archimedes, "and I will move the world." These men moved the world, and so can we all.[30]

The vision referred to in this facet is not the eyesight found in the retina, but rather the metaphorical concept of imagination referred to as "the mind's eye." It involves the capacity of a leader to imagine a preferred future, articulate and clarify that image, and mobilize others toward making it a reality. Marcus Buckingham, in his book, *The One Thing You Need to Know*, emphasizes the significance of great leaders' ability to, rally people to a better future.[31] Vision as a facet of leadership involves having insights about the present and foresight about the future. However, vision building is not a one-person show. Leaders never fulfill a vision alone. Antoine de Saint-Exupery reminds us, "If you want to build a ship, don't herd people together to collect wood and don't assign them tasks and work, but rather teach them to long for the endless immensity of the sea."[32]

There are several aspects of vision that change as the leader moves from level to level. They include its scope, its potential impact, and the degree to which it adds value to the lives of others. In addition to the quality of the vision itself, success in this facet also relies on the ability of the leader to authentically engage others as partners in the journey to fulfillment.

Informed Level: Important

At this level, the leader's vision may be narrow, have a limited impact, and/or contribute value predominantly to the life of the leader. Take, for example, a leader in an automobile manufacturing company who envisions a sleek new design for the next year's model.

This vision extends only to that year and model. It impacts just those who own that car, and because it is strictly a design element, its value is limited to the aesthetic appreciation of consumers and the financial benefits to the leader. Contrast that vision with one of another leader in the same industry who is attempting to convert soy beans into an environmentally safe fuel source. The breadth of his project could encompass potentially all automobiles in the future. It would have worldwide impact and contribute to the environmental welfare of all humanity for centuries.

Leaders at this level may have good but short-term visions. They may also be tenacious in their dedication to a vision that has little potential for impact or contribution to the greater good. At an emotional level, they sincerely want to actualize the vision, but they have not yet reached either the "felt need" or "urgent" emotional levels described in subsequent categories. Additionally, they may not choose or be capable of recruiting others to the cause.

Scripts

"I really want us to be taking this route."

"This is what we need to achieve in the next six months."

"This is the direction we've been given and it is our job to follow this path."

Indicators

- Urgency takes precedence over long-term planning.
- Short-term goals neither inspire nor capture the depth of the mission.
- There are more concerns about the parts than the whole.
- Decisions reflect more reactive than proactive thinking.
- The leader follows the pre-established vision of the organization.

Intentional Level: Significant

In the same way that twisting the lenses of a telescope increases the range and clarity of the object being viewed, the significant category is marked by broader and more defined objectives within the vision of the leader. There is also better clarity about the potential benefit in creating an environment in which the latent need to achieve the vision is awakened in a greater number of people. Honesty, curiosity, and constructive thought are solicited and validated. It is in this kind of environment that people can surface and articulate their previously unspoken concerns in order to assist in the design of a better future. Leaders with a "significant" vision acknowledge the requirement to dedicate substantial time and resources to the enterprise. They also recognize the advantage of enlisting the participation of others to expedite a faster timeline.

Scripts

"Of all the things we could do, what must we do?"
"If not now, when? If not we, who?"
"Clearly this organization is on a new path."
"We're not in Kansas anymore, Dorothy."
"I know this is going to take time, but it's worth it."

Indicators

- The vision statement is written and ready for posting.
- The impact of actions and decisions is noteworthy and lasting.
- The leader collaboratively establishes a clear vision for the part of the organization she leads.
- Recruitment of colleagues to work on the vision is not difficult.

Inspired Level: Historic

A historic vision is characterized as transformational. Literally, historic leadership is so important it alters the history of an organization, a nation, or perhaps even the world. The depth and scope of such a vision translates into the reframing of emotions, thinking, and actions. It might be said, "Things will never be the same." There is a certain degree of "re-ordering" of future events. In order to attain this historic level, leaders must be able to combine all of the elements spoken of in the first two levels (important, significant) and do so at a higher plane. They have more than a felt need; they possess a strong sense of urgency. They offer a vision that is more than clear and compelling; it is so gripping that others enthusiastically volunteer to join in the endeavor without need of recruitment. In the laws of physics, momentum is equal to velocity times mass. Not only are inspired leaders able to garner the necessary mass (human and other resources), but they are also able to maintain the necessary speed. They understand both the importance of the vision and the immediacy of the need to achieve it are required to produce full momentum. This finely tuned sense of timing has been described by Malcolm Gladwell as the "tipping point."[33] He describes the need for a critical mass of concerned individuals in order for a call to action to be effective. This idea was also put forth centuries ago by William Shakespeare. In his play, *Julius Caesar* he said, "There is a tide in the affairs of men, which, when taken at the flood, leads on to fortune. On such a full sea are we now afloat. And we must take the current when it serves, or lose our ventures."[34]

So sophisticated is the skill of inspired visionaries that they are able to recognize the inherent contradictions between their vision and those of others. For instance, the vision of Surgeon General Luther Leonidas Terry, when he issued his warning about the connection between lung cancer and cigarette smoking in 1964, was radically different from that of the tobacco advertising agencies at the same time. Because others were willing to join in the campaign, it was possible to sustain the call to action over time. Almost a half century later, Dr. Terry is credited with launching a historic vision that has expanded to include millions and has resulted in the saving of countless lives.

Though Dr. Terry's historic vision has affected the entire world, each day historic visions are realized of which the world at large is unaware. From a breakthrough in education for reaching autistic children to the articulation of a new concept in a technology lab, the potential for a historic vision exists throughout every profession and organization. Thus, not all historic visions are recorded in encyclopedias or history books. Some are found in the journals of specific trades, small-town newspapers, or simply in the reflective stories passed on verbally from generation to generation throughout our communities. Because these visions are broad in scope, impact significant numbers of people, add value to those they serve, and endure over time, they are historic and so, indeed, are the leaders who have the courage to champion them.

The French Nobel Prize-winning author Andre Gide best captured the spirit of a historic vision when he said, "Look for your own. Do not do what someone else could do as well as you. Do not say, do not write what someone else could say, could write as well as you. Care for nothing in yourself but what you feel exists nowhere else and out of yourself, create, impatiently or patiently ... the most irreplaceable of things."[35]

Scripts:

"We all know what it takes, now let's do it."

"We are only limited by the borders of our imagination."

"This won't be easy, but it will be worth it."

"That action was a turning point in our history."

Indicators:

- Employees agree that what they are engaged in is more than just a day's work. It is a mission.
- Changes in the organization's culture are transformative.
- The leader is relentless in her emphasis on the vision of the organization and the importance of the work in advancing the vision.

Spirit Mover: Courage

Courage is the ability to face danger, difficulty, uncertainty, or pain without being overcome by fear or being diverted from a chosen course of action. Courageous leaders accept the need to embrace the mystery, actively seek the unknown, and accept what may unfold if they are going to realize their vision. Such leaders recognize and capitalize on the earlier described "tipping point" to capture the necessary impetus and move forward. President John F. Kennedy said, "Courage is a magnificent mixture of triumph and tragedy. A man does what he must—in spite of personal consequences; in spite of obstacles and dangers and pressures—and that is the basis of all morality."[36]

An example of an inspirational leader who personified the courage needed to realize a historic vision is Dr. Martin Luther King Jr. King's most influential and well-known public address was the "I Have A Dream" speech, delivered on the steps of the Lincoln Memorial in Washington DC in 1963. In the following excerpts from that speech, one can substitute the word "vision" for "dream" and realize that, clearly, Dr. King was providing Americans with a momentous and compelling image for the future.

I have a (vision) that one day this nation will rise up and live out the true meaning of its creed: "We hold these truths to be self-evident: that all men are created equal."

I have a (vision) that one day on the red hills of Georgia the sons of former slaves and the sons of former slave owners will be able to sit down together at the table of brotherhood.

I have a (vision) that my four little children will one day live in a nation where they will not be judged by the color of their skin but by the content of their character.[37]

Dr. King's leadership required courage with a degree of risk that most leaders are never asked to face—the risk of his life. On that day, he spoke before more than a quarter of a million people, knowing that among the multitude, there could be one who would try to kill him. Though the assassination did not occur on that historic day, it did, indeed, happen on April 4, 1968, on the balcony of the Lorraine Motel in Memphis, Tennessee.

Most leaders will thankfully not have to risk their lives to advance their dreams for a better future. But *every* vision requires courage, especially when faced with the greatest adversary to progress—the fear of the unknown. Jonas Salk, developer of a polio vaccine in the 1950s, commented, "Hope lies in dreams, in imagination, and in the courage of those who dare to make dreams into reality."[38]

RSVP

Reflect on your vision. Does it have the potential to be historic? If not, modify it so it can be and discuss your modifications with others.

Quotation:

"The people of the world can live together in peace. We know that is God's vision. We have the power to make the world we seek, but only if we have the courage to make a new beginning."[39]
—President Barack Obama. Address at Cairo University in Egypt. June 4, 2009

Spirit Movers: Attributes for Transforming Leadership

Elaborated Rubric for the Facet of Vision

FACET	Informed (Prepared Way)	Intentional (Purposeful Way)	Inspired (Passionate Way)
Vision	Important	Significant	Historic
Standard: *The leader has the capacity to imagine a preferred future; articulate and clarify that image; and mobilize others toward making it a reality.*	The leader's image of the future is narrow and/or has limited impact and/or is short term. The leader's ability to recruit others may be limited.	The leader's image of the future is broad, has recognizable importance and extends beyond the leader's tenure. Others can be recruited to participate in efforts to achieve the vision.	The leader's image of the future is comprehensive, compelling, and has the potential for profound impact. Others share the passion of the leader and enthusiastically volunteer to be involved.
The Spirit Mover Is Courage.	Organizational Indicators:	Organizational Indicators:	Organizational Indicators:
	• Urgency trumps long-range planning. • Decisions are predominantly reactive in nature. • There are more concerns for the parts than the whole.	• The vision is known by all. • Substantial time and resources are dedicated to the vision. • Honesty, curiosity, and constructive thought are sought and valued.	• Changes in the organization's culture are transformative. • Time and resources that advance the vision are given priority. • The significance of the vision is stronger than any individual.

Chapter 7

The Facet of Talent

*"Your talent is God's gift to you. What you do with it is
your gift back to God"*[40]
—Leo Buscaglia, Author

Standard: **The leader refines and focuses his natural ability
in order to capitalize on his gifts for a higher good.**

There are two definitions of the word *talent* that are useful
as we try to distinguish the leadership levels in this facet. In
today's society, the term *talent* refers to a person's natural ability
to capitalize on his or her gifts. This definition serves as the first
way to differentiate among the levels of talent. It is the degree
to which leaders devote themselves to improving their ability to
lead. However, commitment to the refinement of one's talent is
only one part of the equation.

There is a second definition of talent that is equally important.
In several ancient civilizations, talent referred to "any of several
units of weight or money." The application of this very old
meaning to the current leadership context suggests it is not only

important to dedicate oneself to developing talent, but it is also critical to examine how that talent will be "spent." What weight will the leader place upon the choices that avail themselves each day? In order to assess his appropriate placement on the rubric in the Facet of Talent, the leader must be able to answer two questions: "To what degree of my capacity have I honed my talent?" and "To what end am I applying it?"

Informed Level: Developed

Leadership, like a growing tree, must have nutrients to enable it to grow stronger. Successful growth in leadership skills is nurtured by humility and tenacity. Humility recognizes and welcomes the existence of a vast body of knowledge and empirical wisdom to be drawn upon. Tenacity affords the energy to pursue knowledge and practice its application in leadership situations.

Informed leaders are stable and reliable in the improvement and application of their talent. They are attentive to their own leadership development and receptive to mastering new strategies. Like trained craftsmen, they have learned to use the proven tools of their trade and do so routinely. They prepare themselves for the changes in the position they currently fill. Though often described as *solid* in their leadership, they may also be depicted as *fluid* in their focus. At this level, leaders have developed the talent to lead and recognize the importance of service, but it remains for them to forge the intricate link that allows them to combine the two and consciously live out their talent in service to others.

Scripts

"I've been given an opportunity to lead, and I can do this."

"I've got what it takes."

"I've done this task before, and I can do it with my eyes closed."

Indicators

- The potential for application of talent is not fully realized.
- Focus is on preparation and competence.
- They are not forward looking in their professional development, choosing rather to become more proficient at their current position.

Intentional Level: Dedicated

Focus and sacrifice characterize leaders at this level. Their commitment to leadership development often results in denial of personal interests. These are the leaders who are often the first ones at work and the last to leave the office. They are likely to read professional publications rather than fiction and welcome input about their performance in an effort to improve. They become highly skilled and are often the authors of new programs and ideas. These leaders are more proactive than their colleagues at the *informed level* and prepare themselves to contribute to their profession, regardless of their position. As master craftsmen, they go beyond the "blueprint," inserting singular workmanship into their leadership. The refinement of their talent is a goal in itself.

Scripts

"I'll do whatever it takes."

"To me, leadership is my passion, and I will never stop trying to improve myself as a leader."

"I am proud to be a career _____."

Indicators

- They often conduct seminars that leaders at the *informed level* are likely to attend.

- Benefits to the profession transcend individual wants and needs.
- They have difficulty slipping away from the job.
- Their personhood is defined by their work.
- People describe their leaders as tenacious.
- Contributions to the profession go beyond one's position.

Inspired Level: Endowed

Inspired leaders see leadership as more than an end in itself. Their mission and the people for whom they lead define their lives. They view their ability to lead others as an endowment. Further, they feel a core responsibility to use their gifts with the same generosity of spirit with which they believe they were given. Consequently, they constantly seek to improve both their art and their level of service.

Like informed leaders, they are good students. Like intentional leaders, they are singular in the application of their talent. In addition, at this level they possess a broader view of the world and see their service rather than themselves at its center. In keeping with the metaphor of the craftsman, these leaders would apply their skill in building a home for Habitat for Humanity. They prepare themselves for the possibilities life offers them to contribute to the greater good, regardless of position or profession.

Some people are happiest when they receive gifts. As such, their joy is forever contingent upon the will of others. But as Mortimer Adler said, "Love consists of giving without getting in return—in giving what is not owed, what is not due the other."[41] Those leaders who are happy when empowering others through their talents are destined to live a positive paradox: they enhance their capacities to give by getting, and they get by giving. Their energy is cyclical. Simply stated, inspired leaders love what their leadership talent can do for others. They are consistently striving for full attainment of their capacity.

Scripts

> "I view my talent for leadership as a gift that should be used for the good of others."
> "I'm happiest when the gifts of others add value beyond measure."
> "I celebrate daily how much others contribute to our total success."

Indicators

- Creativity and high energy in the leader and others are the standards.
- They determine if a specific conference would advance the mission and send the most logical person, which may or may not be themselves.
- The positive impact of their talent is pervasively evident.
- The impact of the talent exceeds the typical boundaries and expectations of the profession.

Spirit Mover: Passion

Leaders with highly developed abilities and clearly defined foci are poised to be effective. Like flint and steel, they are ineffective when held separately. It is the leader's passion that brings them together to ignite the flames of true leadership. Our intention for using passion as a Spirit Mover for the Facet of Talent is well captured by a quote from Field Marshal Ferdinand Foch, French military theorist, who said, "The most powerful weapon on earth is the human soul on fire."[42]

Passion provides the impetus that allows a leader to move from level to level in this facet. The passion of a developed leader is refined, but often dormant and understated. At the *dedicated level*, that passion is self-evident and articulated. This means that the leader is internally aware of his/her passion and is also able to articulate it in terms that others can clearly understand. At the highest level, the leader's passion speaks for itself. Those who view their talent as an endowment recognize it as a means to an end. They use their passion to establish a powerful momentum toward their ultimate goal of service.

As one's passion for one's talent increases from level to level, the need for results and impact becomes more important. Self-sacrifice might be a factor as the dedication is shifted from self to others or a larger goal.

Another way to view passion as a Spirit Mover is to ask the questions, "If someone is truly passionate, what does it look like? What is evident when someone is passionate about his or her talent?" Three concepts or variables come to mind: focus, energy, and time commitment. Intensity in these variables is exhibited consistently and is quite evident. Also, the passion for one's talent is so integrated into personality, decisions, and choices that there is no pretense or second guessing; it is simply a part of one's nature. A leader at the *inspired level* of talent exhibits all of these qualities.

When the desire to exercise one's talent is so compelling it reaches the *inspired level*, it is no longer confined within the individual. It has become an integrated part of the workings of humanity. The leader's passion extends beyond his own talent. As Curt Coffman, co-author of *Follow this Path* points out, "Great managers think that excellence should be revered in every job. They see their task as defining the talent needed for every roll, and then choosing the appropriately talented person for that role.

This way, the person does what he or she does best every day."[43]
Passion for one's talent is, in a very positive way, contagious.

RSVP

What talent do you have that holds the potential to be your greatest legacy? State specifically how your current work is contributing to your desired legacy and what new actions you must take.

Quotation:

"Only passions, great passions, can elevate the soul to great things."[44]
—Denis Diderot, French philosopher

Spirit Movers: Attributes for Transforming Leadership

Elaborated Rubric for the Facet of Talent

FACET	Informed (Prepared Way)	Intentional (Purposeful Way)	Inspired (Passionate Way)
Talent	Developed	Dedicated	Endowed
Standard: *The leader refines and focuses his natural ability in order to capitalize on his gifts for a higher good.*	They are attentive to their own leadership development and receptive to new strategies. Service to others may occur, but is a coincidental outcome.	They are attentive to organizational development and author new programs and ideas. Service to others is evidenced.	They are attentive to their purpose in life and the potential of their talent, at its highest level, to achieve it. Service to others is fundamental and consistent.
The Spirit Mover Is Passion.	**Organizational Indicators** <ul><li>Focus is on preparation and competence.</li><li>The potential for application of talent is not fully realized.</li><li>They are not forward looking in their professional development, choosing rather to become more proficient at their current position.</li></ul>	**Organizational Indicators:** <ul><li>Benefits to the profession transcend individual wants and needs.</li><li>Refinement of talent is a goal in itself.</li><li>Leaders are described as tenacious.</li><li>Contributions to the profession go beyond one's position.</li></ul>	**Organizational Indicators:** <ul><li>Creativity and high energy in the leader and others are the standards.</li><li>Positive impact of their talent is pervasively evident.</li><li>The impact of the talent exceeds the typical boundaries of the profession.</li></ul>

Chapter 8

The Facet of Change

"Progress occurs when courageous, skillful leaders seize the opportunity to change things for the better."[45]
—Harry S. Truman, 33rd U. S. President

S*tandard:* **The leader orchestrates the organization's future direction and is persistent in staying the course.**

Simply stated, "to change" means "to become or make something different." But change is far from a simple process. Within the context of leadership, multiple variables exist that make leading change a challenging endeavor. Among these variables are: the number of changes being implemented at one time; the speed at which the changes must happen; the intricacy of the changes; and the effects of the changes on people and relationships. Each of these variables adds a layer of difficulty to the role of the leader. Daunting though it may be, it is impossible to avoid the change process. We are reminded of an old paradox: "Change is the only constant." Therefore, "To change or not to change" is really not the question. The only choices that exist are between influencing the direction of change or being relegated to the role of respondent to the changes brought about by others. To make a difference, a leader must embrace change as inevitable and seek the positive possibilities that change can bring. Those with faith in a better future have an innate need to add definition to their optimism by crystallizing and articulating the need for specific change(s). Leaders with faith must also have the persistence necessary to guide others on the road that must be traveled.

Reflecting on many enlightening books about the phenomenon of change has served to inform us as we write this book. Our mentors in print have included: William F. Bridges, Rosabeth Moss Kanter, Michael Fullan, John P. Kotter, Spencer Johnson, Kenneth Blanchard, Margaret Wheatley, and numerous others. From our readings, and the empirical learnings of our experiences, we have found a number of common threads that consistently emerge as challenges to those who attempt to lead others through change processes. Five of the most prevailing of these challenges which the leader must face in himself and in others are:

1. Reluctance to leave the status quo
2. Fear of the unknown
3. Endurance to persevere over time
4. The pessimism of naysayers and skeptics
5. Fear of the consequences of failure.

Because the three levels in the Facet of Change (contentment, curiosity, and commitment) are based on the way leaders confront these challenges, we believe a brief examination of each is imperative before moving on. We chose to do this through the use of a metaphor.

Change As a Board Game

In this game, there are five rooms through which leaders must pass in order to successfully navigate the pathway to change. The goal of the game is to achieve the desired transformation without residual damage to the organization or its people.

The first room is known as the "Comfort Zone" (status quo). In this climate-controlled space, the leader is secure, protected by the invisible walls of security and predictability. Only when the leader can articulate a reason for change more compelling than the comfort of the status quo will he exit this room and move further down the hall.

In direct contrast to the transparency of the "Comfort Zone," the second room is the "Dark Room" (the unknown). Its contents are mysterious and may arouse fears and concerns about the negative developments that could lie within. When the leader can make uncertainty his friend and embrace the positive potential within the unknown and untried, he can move forward once again.

Room 3 is the Fitness Center. Any change, no matter how small, requires energy (endurance) to implement. Leaders who are not willing to commit the physical and emotional energy needed to get through this room may be forced to exit through a side door to reevaluate their role as a change agent.

The "Doubting Thomas Board Room" is the sign over the door of Room Three. A meeting is in session as the leader enters. He is required to seat himself at the head of the table and listen to the Thomases (Naysayers and Skeptics) as they list *all* the reasons why the change might fail. The leader is required to give honest consideration to every comment. If new and convincing reasons are presented to abort the change process, the leader must retreat to the Comfort Zone with all of the Thomases. If, however, he can weigh all issues and concerns with compassion and without losing either confidence or focus on the potential positive outcomes of the change, he may move on down the hall.

The fifth and final room, called the "Status Room" (fear of the consequences of failure), contains a very tall ladder. When the leader enters, he is placed on a rung partway up the ladder. He is informed that if this change doesn't work out well, he may have to descend to a lower rung and perhaps even start over again at the bottom. On the other hand, success could result in a step up. If the leader is willing to accept the risk of failing as an inherent part of the change process and become comfortable with that knowledge, he has earned passage through the final door.

As he exits the fifth and final door, the leader finds he is in familiar territory once again positioned at the entrance to the "Comfort Zone." He realizes that the Change Game is on a round board because, like change itself, this game is never-ending. As rewards for completing the cycle, the leader is given one Confidence Chip and one Credibility Chip. The Confidence Chip can be used to shorten the time spent in the Dark Room in ensuing cycles while Credibility Chips may each be spent to eliminate one Doubting Thomas from the Board Room.

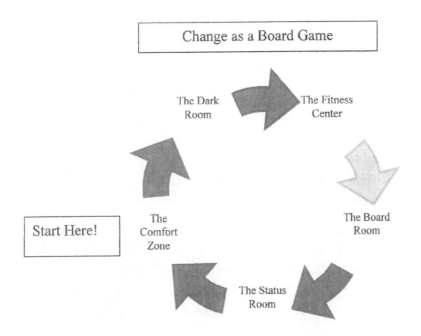

The manner in which leaders confront the aforementioned challenges determines their placement on the following levels of the facet of change: contentment, curiosity, and commitment.

Informed Level: Contentment

Contentment is often characterized by self-satisfaction. A contented leader is usually unreflective and without awareness of either dangers or possibilities. The primary concerns of leaders who function at this level are safety and tranquility. The desire to be secure and stay in the status quo is common here. The work of leadership is habitual in some ways. Therefore, when one is at the level of contentment, he doesn't question the merits and value of change but rather feels the weight of being asked to think or do things differently. Resistance to difference in habits and routines results in a virtual bondage of self.

Such leaders fail to acknowledge change as ever-present in the landscape of leadership. All leaders must come to grips with the degree to which they desire and inspire change in themselves and in others. Anchored by fear of negative impact on the organization or on personal status, leaders who are content are rarely tempted to initiate change. Rather, they respond to changes initiated by others.

When there is lack of clarity and context in the direction or meaning of change it is more comfortable to stay the course. Additionally, the absence of knowledge and skills necessary to be effective in a new situation makes it difficult to embrace change and take risks. Leaders at this level may need to develop within themselves and subsequently in those they lead the willingness to seek and give more information. Professional development is key to arm people with needed skills.

A prompting message for those at the level of contentment is provided by Margaret Wheatley in her book, *Turning to One Another*. She states, "I think the greatest source of courage is to realize that if we don't act, nothing will change for the better. Reality doesn't change itself. It needs us to act."[46] There is no substitute for confidence in oneself in the realization of a desired change. Only those leaders who understand and overcome the lure of temporary predictability that characterizes the status quo and endeavor to take those risks are those who are able to move on to the next level.

Scripts:

"Where are we going with this change?"

"We've got a good thing going, let's not ruin it."

"We tried that years ago. It didn't work then either."

"Are we sure this is worth the risk?"

"I know what needs to be done, but I don't think I have the skills to make it happen."

"I don't think I have the energy to deal with the assaults from the contrarians."

Indicators

- The leader does not initiate or fully and genuinely participate in reform efforts.
- Continuity rather than creativity is celebrated.
- Changes in schedules and routines are resisted.
- There are limited communications related to the vision and mission.
- Hiring of risk-takers is rarely evident.
- There is no invitation to ask good questions.

Intentional Level: Curiosity

Curiosity refers to eagerness to know about something or to get more information about it. There is a wonderful expression used to describe persons in this category. They learn to live in the mystery. Additionally they lean into the discomfort and exhibit a willingness to initiate deliberate risk. These leaders can see the possibilities of success and are available to new thinking. They calculate the degree of jeopardy as measured against the degree of potential and take a route balancing the two. At this stage, leaders are willing to withhold judgment about the value of the change. They are comfortable in a state of suspension (the unknown) for a period of time, and they possess an attitude of availability. They welcome new ideas from others and enjoy the process of pondering possibilities. Conversely, those who *remain* at this level are known for not following through (endurance) and therefore, real change never occurs.

How do leaders facilitate a sense of curiosity in self and others? How can they make themselves and others better guardians of the change processes? We posed these questions to leaders in one of our client organizations. As a result of deeper conversations related to processes, programs, and patterns of implementation efforts, the leaders articulated ways and behaviors they could adopt to indeed be better guardians of the change process.

They included:

- Have intentional conversations about change as a process.
- Broaden the base and make sure individuals understand any change initiative and their role in implementation.
- Keep recognizing, developing, and using the capacity of internal personnel to assist others in becoming more effective agents of change.
- Develop a participatory process to communicate, implement, and evaluate change initiative.
- Provide continuous support and follow-through before, during, and after a change initiative.
- Celebrate and tell the story of previous successes.

The above examples have the potential to fuel the desire for meaningful change and assist individuals in moving through the three levels of change as a Facet of Leadership: contentment, curiosity, and courage.

Scripts

"Before I ask others to change, I had better ask what is sacred around here."

"What if …"

"Have you ever considered …"

"I'm excited to see where this change could lead us."

"What are they doing in other organizations about this?"
"Surely there's a better way."

Indicators

- Adaptability is valued.
- New ideas are welcomed given serious consideration.
- A large network of colleagues is maintained and drawn upon for their expertise and experiences.
- The leader constantly seeks to understand best practices based upon sound research.

Inspired Level: Commitment

The power of commitment was expressed by the German writer and philosopher Johan Wolfgang Von Goethe when he observed, "The moment one definitely commits oneself, then providence moves too. Whatever you can do or dream you can, begin it. Boldness has genius, power and magic in it."[47] In the context of change, we see commitment in the same light as the boldness described by Goethe. We believe commitment to be the powerful combination of convictions and confidence. This translates into dedication. When self-knowledge (convictions) combines with self-assurance (confidence), the highest level of commitment and the greatest potential for meaningful change is the result.

The level of commitment required of the leader is affected by both the size of the change and the degree to which it represents a departure from the status quo.

A change which could be characterized as a "tweak" of an accepted practice will require far less energy than that which would be viewed as a "radical departure." Similarly, a change that impacts a limited number of people or resources may be accepted more quickly.

It is our belief that changes of significance should not be initiated and then delegated to others. Though the work required to implement the change can and should be shared the leader must maintain active and focused involvement or face the risk that the change process will lose momentum or even be abandoned.

One case in point involves the issue of global warming. Countless scientists and world leaders had attempted to alert the citizenry of the world about the dangers of global warming in the past, but their efforts were inconsistent and/or their work underfunded. It was the committed leadership of former Vice President Al Gore, including the Academy Award-winning motion picture, *An Inconvenient Truth,* that raised the collective conscience of the world to a much higher level. He received the Nobel Prize for Peace along with the United Nations' Intergovernmental Panel on Climate Change. The IPCC includes twenty-five hundred researchers from over 130 nations. But it was Gore's singular efforts that were recognized in the official Nobel Citation which read," He is probably the single individual who has done the most to create worldwide understanding of the measures that need to be adopted.".

Other illustrations of the highest level of commitment to a vision include such historic projects as the lunar landing, the civil rights movement, and the fight against AIDS. However, the designation is not limited to those widely known and publicized events. Countless leaders have championed important changes within the context of their own realities and remained unnoticed and uncelebrated by the broader public. Every profession has within it those who possess the diligence, timing, and unyielding conviction to lead others to a better future.

Rosabeth Moss Kanter would say people at this level are "Change Masters: those people who are adept at the art of anticipating the need for, and of leading, productive change."[48] In contrast to the other levels, committed leaders determine their choices based upon the potential for the good of all. Having once committed to a change, they do not allow such factors as political correctness or magnitude of effort to mitigate their diligence and perseverance. Author Marcus Buckingham said, "If great managers are catalysts, speeding up the reaction between the individual's talents and the company's goals, then great leaders are alchemists. Somehow they are able to transform fear of the unknown into confidence in the future."[49]

Scripts

"I must remember to realize and respect people walk the world in different ways."

"Anything worth having is worth fighting for."

"This is more important than the job."

"To stay the same is to go backward over time."

"I have a dream."

"I wonder who I will become as a result of leading this change."

"This is what my life's journey is all about."

Indicators

- Standing up for the change even if it is controversial is characteristic of the leader.
- Resources to fund change are sought, when none are readily available through normal channels.
- Thoughtful risk taking is valued.
- Providing professional growth opportunities, incentives, and rewards to those who participate in significant change is a part of the culture.

- People feel energized and empowered throughout the organization.
- There is pride in both the change process and outcomes.

Spirit Mover: Optimism

There is an old proverb that says, "If I keep a green bough in my heart, a singing bird will come." Optimistic leaders not only keep a metaphorical bough in their hearts, but they also extend it to those with whom they work. We believe that informed optimism is the absolute underpinning of any effective change process. "Informed optimism" is different from "blind optimism" in the sense that it is anchored in both reality and possibility.

It is optimism that moves leaders from the comfort of contentment, through the intrigues of curiosity, and ultimately to the possibilities of courage.

In order to understand the spirit of optimism, it is helpful to contrast it with its antithesis, pessimism. An optimist believes that the world is evolving for the best and will ultimately result in the greatest good. One familiar and popular credo of optimism is Max Ehrmann's poem, "Desiderata" in which he advises, "You are a child of the universe, no less than the trees and the stars, you have a right to be here. And whether or not it is clear to you, the universe is unfolding as it should.[50]" Conversely, pessimism is the opinion that everything in nature will result in the worst possible outcome. Oscar Wilde offered another definition. He said, "A pessimist is one who, when he has the choice of two evils, chooses both."[51]

In the realm of leadership, it is clear that a culture of optimism must be evident in order for any change to be successfully conceived, implemented, and maintained. When faced with a need for a change, a pessimistic leader displays his perennial "doubting Thomas" attitude. The negativity of such individuals results in constant barriers to the change process. In a time when changes are abundant, rapid, and stressful, leading people out of the comfort of the status quo and into the uncertainty of change is at best a challenge.

By contrast, optimists are bolstered by three constant companions: hope, confidence, and passion. Their hope is manifest in their predisposition to see a better life ahead; their confidence enables them to act on that vision; and their passion is the fuel they need to persevere. Realistically, hope, confidence, and passion, without discipline and action, hold hollow promise for the desired change.

Optimists do not embrace change for change's sake. While they recognize that change is a dominant force in the world today, they refuse to allow it to dominate either their mission or the people they serve. Optimistic leaders are able to bring clarity to both the specifics of the change and the benefits of its completion. This enables them to recruit the courage of others that, when compounded with their own courage, gives powerful and positive momentum to the course of change.

RSVP

In what area of your personal or professional life is change so vital that you are beyond curiosity and willing to invest your commitment? Carpe diem! Seize the day.

Quotation:

"Perpetual optimism is a force multiplier."[52]
—Colin Powell

Spirit Movers: Attributes for Transforming Leadership

Elaborated Rubric for the Facet of Change

FACET	Informed (Prepared Way)	Intentional (Purposeful Way)	Inspired (Passionate Way)
Change	**Contentment**	**Curiosity**	**Commitment**
The leader's desire to orchestrate the organization's future direction and his persistence in staying the course.	The leader prefers the comfort and predictability of the status quo. He is *reactive* in terms of change and his responses are short term in duration.	The leader is willing to experiment. He *actively* engages in the change process and may also support long-term changes. Difficulty in implementation or new data could cause abandonment of the process before completion.	The leader is *proactive* in his search for changes that will improve the conditions and/or advance the mission of the organization. Once committed to a change, he is tenacious about bringing the process to completion.
The Spirit Mover Is Optimism.	**Organizational Indicators:**	**Organizational Indicators:**	**Organizational Indicators:**
	• Continuity is celebrated rather than creativity. • Leader does not initiate or participate in reform efforts. • Leader is sometimes viewed as a pessimist. • Leader resists changes in schedules and routines.	• New ideas are welcome. • The leader supports experiments with discretionary resources. • The leader seeks best practices based on sound research. • Adaptability is valued.	• The leader empowers others to co-create. • The leader stands up for change even if it is controversial. • A focus exists on creative funding. • Thoughtful risk taking is valued.

Chapter 9

The Facet of Time

*"Time is the coin of your life. It is the only coin you have,
and only you can determine how it will be spent. Be careful
lest you let other people spend it for you."*[53]
—Carl Sandburg, Poet

Standard: **The leader uses both the quantity and quality of his time to advance the mission and vision of the organization.**

The heart of this facet is related to the choices that are made within the available time. Effective leaders are able to discriminate among their many options and select those that resonate within their souls and connect directly and meaningfully to their core mission and vision and the organization's as well. In addition to making decisions about the *quantity* of time spent on a given task, leaders must also be consciously thoughtful about the *quality* of their time. We recognize that there will be some fluctuation among the levels in the Facet of Time when situational leadership is required. However, even when circumstances demand different timelines, leaders still tend to function in the way that feels most natural to them.

Though people within an organization may not have access to the leader's calendar or intentions, they can often determine his level of function in the Facet of Time by examining his countenance. "Countenance" refers to the way a person presents himself—his demeanor or comportment. Such nonverbal signals clearly reflect the leader's view of time as one of the following: a commodity to spend efficiently (Expeditious); an important variable to control in order to achieve an objective (Goal Setting); or an ever-present context within which to realize heartfelt priorities (Soul Fulfilling).

Informed Level: Expeditious

At this level, the facet of time is characterized by reactivity. Urgency takes precedence over a task's relative importance in the long range. The emphasis is on time management. Leaders in this category try to accommodate all requests for their time and, in the process, render themselves incapable of devoting enough attention to any of them.

Their lack of prioritization results in sporadic decisions, inconsistent results, and frustration for others in the organization.

The countenance of a leader at this level is frequently frenetic and marked by nervous energy. Rather than appearing focused and in control, this leader is often found watching the clock, checking text messages, and calling abrupt endings to meetings. Because he tends to have too many irons in the fire, this leader is sometimes described as a jack of all trades.

The positive aspect of operating expeditiously or "in the moment" is the ability to respond to an immediate crisis.

Long-range planning may suffer, but when spontaneity and/or multi-tasking are needed, this leader is often able to provide it. Important examples are first responders and front-line soldiers whose ability to reason and act quickly is essential to save lives.

Scripts

"I'm on it. We need to take care of this right now."

"That will have to wait. This is more critical."

"Okay, listen up, this is an emergency, and this is what we need to do."

"For now, let's just go ahead and schedule it."

Indicators

- The last people to make a request usually get what they want.
- Emergencies and crises are handled well, though poor planning may have caused some of them.
- Appointments are often double-scheduled and canceled.
- Personal stress is increased by attempts to do it all.

Intentional Level: Goal Setting

This level is about time improvement. It is the conscious study of the use of time and how to improve its use based on pre-established goals. Time improvement is purposeful, strategic, and usually related to mission values and roles, personal or professional. Leaders at this level make the most of time by reducing the amount of effort spent on tasks that do not contribute to the vision/mission.

Intentional leaders view time as a precious commodity, and they guard it tenaciously. They reserve their time for needed projects, desired outcomes, and important achievements. As opposed to the first level where leaders tend to operate in the moment, here the leader focuses on quality, not speed. Precision in timelines, calendars, and agendas, etc., all reflect this leader's frugal expenditure of the resource of time.

The countenance of a goal-setting leader is highly focused. Unlike the leader who is easily distracted by interruptions, this leader keeps his eyes on the prize and demands the same of others. He is likely to come to meetings with charts, graphs, and other data relevant to his priorities. He is conservative about adding any new topics to the agenda.

The obvious strength of leaders at this level is their capacity to get things done. They are very precise and judicious about their use of time on task and their expectations of others. Of them it is often said, "If you want the job done and done right, he's your man."

Scripts

"I need to go because I have another commitment, and I don't want to keep people waiting."

"I'd like us all to analyze our expenditures for last year in relation to our goals. Did we put our resources of time where our mouth was?"

"What is the best use of our time to move the mission forward?"

Indicators

- Daily long- and short-range planning calendars/devices are used.
- Priorities are clear and understood by others.
- Time use is a topic of reflection and is subject to ongoing refinement.

Inspired Level: Soul-Fulfilling

The time facet at this level is about time fulfillment and answers the question, "In the grand scheme of things, is this really what matters most? In what ways does it have heart and meaning for us?" Leaders have an earnest dedication to creating a better future focused on possibilities. At this level there is appropriate mastery of delegation. Minutiae and redundancies, which can be large consumers of time, are minimized, enabling the leader to make the most of his day by focusing on those matters that contribute to the vision/mission.

In *Thinking in Time: The Uses of History for Decision Making,* Richard Neustad writes about the importance of viewing time as a stream. He shows the way lessons learned from the past, when applied to the present, can profoundly affect the future.[54] George Santayana said, "Those who cannot remember the past are condemned to repeat it."[55] One has only to reverse that point of view to surmise that *remembering* the lessons of the past means that the mistakes of the past *are less likely to be* repeated. It is an unconscionable waste of time to reinvent wheels. High-functioning leaders recognize their own diminutive position in relation to the stream of time. This important perspective of time as a stream adds breadth and context to their decisions.

Leaders at this level have calmer countenances than their expeditious (tense) or goal-setting (intense) colleagues. Their ability to view time in its greater perspective allows them to be less affected by minor issues or a *crisis du jour* that may distract others. Secure in their clarity of purpose, these leaders are sometimes referred to as "old souls" or "wise for their age."

In order to achieve "Soul Fulfilling" status, in the Facet of Time, the leader must be able to make the conscious connection of time with closely held and valued priorities. Time is prized for its potential to improve the well-being of self and others and becomes a vehicle for twenty-first-century philanthropy. An inspired leader will marshal and focus the discretionary time available within the organization, directing it toward projects that are helpful to the communities they serve. The soul-fulfilled leader is a steadfast student of history, an observant participant in the present, and an optimistic voyager into the future.

Scripts

"If we do this, how will it affect the future of our mission?"

"Forget the numbers for a minute. What is your heart telling you?"

"I know I would enjoy meeting with you, but that's really my assistant's area, and I am confident she will do a great job for you."

"Time is precious and fleeting, so let's use it wisely."

Indicators

- Research is a constant in all planning processes.
- People know who to go to, depending on the issue and the task.
- Meetings are exciting and focus on positive possibilities for the future.
- The leader maximizes a time management system at the highest level in order to lead and serve others more effectively.

Spirit Mover: Discernment

Discernment is the Spirit Mover for the Facet of Time. William Jennings Bryan counseled, "Destiny is not a matter of chance, it is a matter of choice; it is not a thing to be waited for, it is a thing to be achieved."[56] We believe in order to make good choices among the countless opportunities that present themselves each day, a leader must be able to discern those that have heart and meaning from those that do not. Leaders who are at the *informed level* wait for circumstance to dictate their use of time. Leaders who are intentional have clearly set goals and prioritize their time to focus on those goals. Clearly, discernment comes to the prepared mind. These are leaders who are inspired do more than respond to or prioritize their time. They take the advice of Horace and "carpe diem;" they seize the day to create their own destinies. Such leaders possess a high level of consciousness about their deepest convictions and principles. They are able to articulate a personal and professional manifesto—a declaration of the principles and objectives they hold most dear. Consequently, leaders at the *inspired level* are able to discern the course of action which will have the greatest impact and focus their time and energies in ways that will help them and the organization they serve to actualize their beliefs. Thus, in times of reflection, they have fewer instances of "I wish I had …" and more "I'm glad I did."

RSVP

Time has two dimensions, quantity and quality. Examine your calendar appointments for the next month (quantity). Do they reflect the second dimension of time (quality)? If necessary, rearrange your time in order to ensure that your work holds heart and meaning.

Quotation:

> *"The supreme end of education is expert discernment in all things—the power to tell the good from the bad, the genuine from the counterfeit, and to prefer the good and the genuine to the bad or the counterfeit."*[57]
> —Samuel Johnson

Spirit Movers: Attributes for Transforming Leadership
Elaborated Rubric for the Facet of Time

FACET	Informed (Prepared Way)	Intentional (Purposeful Way)	Inspired (Passionate Way)
Time	Expeditious	Goal Setting	Soul Fulfilling
Standard: *The leader uses both the quantity and quality of his time to advance the mission and vision of the organization.*	The leader's focus is on the present. Crisis management is the priority. The leader tries to respond to all requests of her time without prioritizing.	The leader's focus is on future timelines and specific goals. The leader emphasizes time allocated to tasks that are directly related to the goals and plans of the organization.	The leader views time as a resource critical to the advancement of the priorities and possibilities for the organization and the people it impacts. Time is consciously connected with the organization's vision.
	Organizational Indicators:	**Organizational Indicators:**	**Organizational Indicators:**
The Spirit Mover is Discernment	Emergencies are handled well Appointments are often cancelled. Agendas are constructed to deal with immediate issues. The last person to make a request usually gets what they want.	Organizational priorities are commonly understood. Agendas are predictable and reflect the organization's goals.. The way time is used is the topic of reflection and discussion within the organization.	Time, itself, is spent pondering the best use of time. Meeting agendas reflect the mission and future potential of the organization. The pursuit of possibilities is emphasized by preserving time for creativity.

Chapter 10

The Facet of Decision Making

"Most discussions of decision-making assume that only senior executives make decisions or that only senior executives' decisions matter. This is a dangerous mistake."[58]
—Peter Drucker, Author

*S*tandard: **The leader drives the actions of the organization by considering content, context and processes.**

All leaders make decisions; it's what they do. In fact, it is such a natural thing that it is easy to assume if enough decisions are made over a long period of time, greater proficiency in decision making will be the result. However, while time and practice can be valuable, they do not guarantee an increase in decisions that are contextually based or wise.

Great leaders are held to a higher standard when it comes to making decisions. Decisions drive actions and actions are at the core of organizational and personal legacies. The leader's task is to discern what must be considered when making any decision, and the leader's values and guiding principles most certainly influence the quality of the decisions.

Informed Level: Isolated

Often, decisions at this level are of convenience and expediency. Urgency may be the driving force for isolated decisions. However, when a leader chooses to adopt a hasty, myopic view of a problem, he limits his perspective to his own singular experience and knowledge. Thereby, he denies himself the expanded thinking that would accompany input from others. Leaders who proactively cultivate a network of wise and willing mentors and advisors to seek out in pressured situations are far less likely to be isolated decision makers.

Another force resulting in isolated decisions is overconfidence. This leader may believe he knows all that is needed to make a decision and feels increased participation will not add value to the decision. An old proverb suggests, "Pride cometh before a fall." Leaders who are too proud to seek input into decisions leave themselves vulnerable to such a fall. A further lesson to be learned from making isolated decisions is the probability that, given no investment by others, the leader is left to deal with the consequences alone.

There is a time and place for isolated decisions and in fact, they can serve the people for whom the decisions are made. An example would be an emergency situation where an immediate command needs to be given and only the leader has the authority and privilege to make that decision.

There are many appropriate, isolated decisions in the realm of personnel issues. For instance, the leader may have to make a decision that involves the firing of an employee and there is no positive purpose to be served by revealing the rationale and facts to a broader audience.

Scripts

"I know this is best and this is what I'm being paid for."

"Ethically, I am not in a position to share this decision."

"I don't have the luxury of time to explain my decision."

Indicators

- Soliciting input is not the norm.
- Those affected by the decision do not necessarily understand the rationale and subsequently have limited ownership.
- Because people function in isolation, there are many conflicts on the master calendar.
- People work at cross purposes.
- Morale is affected when too many decisions are made in isolation.

Intentional Level: Contextual

Intentional leaders understand the value of making decisions within a context involving more than just self. The meaning of the word context (weave together) is paramount in this leader's approach to decision making. Recognizing the value and power of collective intelligence, leaders at his level convene the thinking of those individuals who hold the most information and experience relative to the decision.

In addition to the use of a variety of *human* resources, there is also an obvious and consistent commitment to the use of multiple lenses when examining potential decisions. These might include political realities, social considerations, and fiscal limitations; views of multiple publics; short-term and long-term impacts; etc.

Because a contextual leader's decisions are thoughtful and inclusive, both the leader and the decision are likely to generate a broader base of support than those made in isolation.

We believe leaders who perform at this level would be well served by giving thought to decision making as *both* an art *and* a science. It is enlightening when leaders view their organization as a living organism in a state of continual metamorphosis.

Unfortunately, most people in roles of management and leadership have had little formal training in the anatomy of decision making and its value, significance, and promise. Judgments are deductively analyzed and deemed to be either "good" or "bad." Seldom are decisions rated holistically as "wise" or "unwise" with the deeper question, "What made it so?"

There is an ancient proverb that advises, "Never give a sword to a man who has not learned to dance." Contextual leaders can benefit from understanding how decision making can be more like a dance (a series of rhythmic steps and movements that are orchestrated within the context of a piece of music) than a battle (a drawn-out conflict for dominance).

Scripts

"What is the larger context for this decision?"

"Have I created enough felt need?"

"Is this the best decision for everyone?"

"I wonder if anyone else has had to make this decision."

"Who can help me with this decision?"

Indicators

- Collaboration occurs routinely.
- People believe the decision makes sense.
- One decision does not contradict another.
- There is a lot less "second guessing."

Inspired Level: Wise

In this rubric the third and highest level represents brilliance. "Wise" decisions include more than the breadth of representation and data that characterize the *intentional level*. Wise decisions reflect the broader values of the organization and its people rather than the self-interests of the leader.

Wisdom is more than context; it is context plus depth of experience, cumulative learning, and intuition. The contribution of intuition to wisdom, though difficult to define or measure, is critical. Intuition is viewed as a "knowing" or sixth sense that transcends language. It guides the leader in determining what to do and what not to do—often without the benefit of evidence.

But singular instinct alone is not enough to ensure decisions that are of high value, altruistic, and a-political. To achieve this high level, decisions must have a great deal of thoughtfulness and rigor and may even be unorthodox. Wise decisions may not enjoy either popularity or understanding, but doing the right things right is the dominant motivational force.

The *process* for a wise decision maker is as critical as the *product*. Leaders should not be held hostage to or defined by one decision. However, the process by which decisions are made is fair game for close scrutiny. Decision-making processes must be inclusive, open, consistent, and worthy of trust. Among the voices that should be heard are those who will be affected by the decision, those who will implement the decision and those who have expertise to contribute to the decision. In other words, solid decisions are made close to the action. Once made, decisions must be communicated clearly and supported by the resources necessary to ensure their implementation.

Wise decision makers are those who faithfully reflect on decisions after the fact. Recognizing the limitations of their own humanity, these leaders seek to improve their thinking through constant study combined with the sage counsel of respected friends and colleagues.

Scripts

"What's best for all people?"

"Of all the things we could do, what must we do?"

"I feel this is a moral imperative."

"Because of the humility of our leader, this decision served the greater good."

Indicators

- Decisions reflect thoughtfulness and rigor.
- Diversity of thought, experience, and people are viewed as assets in the organization.
- Intelligence and courage characterize decision makers.

Spirit Mover: Humility

Margaret Wheatley has stated,

"Hopefully, humility leads us up out of our bunkers, to open ground where we step away from the rigidity of our positions and become a bit curious. We need to be open to the possibility that colleagues and even strangers have information and perspectives that may be of value to us."[59]

As illustrated in this statement, a leader's potential for upward movement in the category of decision making is proportional to the degree of humility the leader possesses. Those who make decisions in isolation operate from the "bunkers" described above, while the contextual leader welcomes the "information and perspectives that may be of value." Wise leaders are "open to the possibilities" existing in the universe because they do not see themselves as its center.

Some people believe that humility is the opposite of arrogance. However, the true opposite of arrogance is poor self-esteem. Humility represents the ideal balance between the two. Humble leaders are both confident and unassuming. Confidence is the well from which they draw the desire to lead while modesty is the source of their desire to learn. The authors are in agreement with author and consultant, Curt Coffman, whose belief is that being humble is the most powerful position you can be in as a leader.

RSVP

When were you burned by a decision someone made in isolation? Whom have you scorched lately? How can you repair the burn? Begin the healing today!

Quotation:

"Humility makes great men twice honorable."[60]
—Benjamin Franklin

Spirit Movers: Attributes for Transforming Leadership

Elaborated Rubric for the Facet of Decision Making

FACET	Informed (Prepared Way)	Intentional (Purposeful Way)	Inspired (Passionate Way)
Decision Making	Isolated	Contextual	Wise
Standard: *The leader drives the actions of the organization by considering content, context, and processes.*	Decisions are made within a narrow framework. Thorough consideration of ramifications is absent. The process for making decisions is shallow and irregular.	The commitment exists to use a variety of lenses when making decisions. The leader engages people with multiple values and perspectives. The process is structured.	The intellectual level of the choices made is of high quality. Doing the right thing right is the dominant motivational force. Decision-making process are inclusive, open, consistent, and worthy of trust.
The Spirit Mover Is Courage.	**Organizational Indicators:**	**Organizational Indicators:**	**Organizational Indicators:**
	<ul><li>Input is neither solicited nor valued.</li><li>Limited ownership in decisions due to poor rationale and communications.</li><li>People work at cross purposes.</li></ul>	<ul><li>Collaboration occurs routinely.</li><li>People believe the decision makes sense.</li><li>One decision does not contradict another.</li><li>There is not a lot of "second guessing."</li></ul>	<ul><li>Decisions reflect thoughtfulness and rigor.</li><li>Diversity of thought, experience, and people are assets in the organization.</li><li>Intelligence and courage characterize the decision makers.</li></ul>

Chapter 11

The Facet of Health

"The health of a people is really the foundation upon which all their happiness and all their power as a State depend."[61]
—Benjamin Disraeli, British Prime Minister

S tandard: **The leader establishes a state of personal and/or organizational well being in the physical, intellectual, and emotional dimensions.**

The Oxford English Dictionary describes health as "physical and mental well-being; soundness. Health is different from strength; it is universal good condition."

Within the context of leadership, we view health in a very broad sense to include physical (doing), intellectual (thinking), and emotional (feeling) components. Healthy bodies provide physical strength and energy. Healthy minds generate relevant ideas and insights. Healthy emotions produce a sound mental context for ethical and moral decisions. Effective leaders recognize the importance of maintaining and manifesting a high level in all three dimensions of health. Many, however, address the three dimensions separately. For instance, when it becomes evident that there is a physical illness, the examination of the problem and the subsequent solutions are often isolated from any possible causal relationship within emotional or intellectual realms. It is the integration of *all* that is within that becomes the keystone of holism at the highest level in the Facet of Health.

Informed Level: Resilient

Recognition and response are important skills on which a resilient leader in the category of health relies. They know the importance of their active involvement in their organization and are alert, even at the early stages, to recognize any health issues that might take them away from those they serve. These leaders, with the help of a repertoire of strategies and resources, are able to bounce back quickly from setbacks caused by any health issue.

Physical

At the *informed level*, a person with a physical illness will gather the appropriate medications, rest, and treat, rather than avoid the symptoms. Their resiliency is based on prompt and proper attention to the malady at hand.

Intellectual

Intellectual health in leadership is not about the *degree* of aptitude as measured by an IQ test. Rather, in its expanded perspective, intelligence also includes the way leaders consciously *use* their intellect to provide the broadest possible framework for their actions. At the *informed level*, the leader, when faced with an issue, will respond by gathering information and engaging in conversations that will increase his or her knowledge bank to handle the issue effectively.

Emotional

There are countless reasons why a leader may encounter emotional stress. For instance, it is possible to become so consumed by work that depression or anxiety may result.

At the *informed level*, a person who is depressed or anxious will recognize the symptoms and search for ways to eliminate them. Their responses could range from simply increasing time spent in relationships and activities proven to elevate their emotional outlook to seeking the services of a medical professional.

Scripts

"I don't know the answer, but I'm going online to see if I can find some data on that topic."

"I'll be fine. I just need a little rest."

"I need to take better care of myself. Reaching out to family, having more recreation, and reading for pleasure would all be helpful."

Indicators

- Quick fixes are sought to get over physical illnesses.
- Leaders give little consideration to the underlying causes of the health issue, just the temporary cure.
- The frequency of sick days throughout the organization is above the norm.
- Wellness programs are lacking in the organization.
- Problems are not ignored but may not be dealt with in a timely fashion.

Intentional Level: Proactive

The key to proactivity lies in the leader's capacity to anticipate and prepare for issues and situations yet to come. Exploring potential options can be very helpful at this level.

Physical

At this level, the leader attempts to prevent the onset of disease or illness by following a regimen that builds up resistance and immunity. Efforts at prevention might include a vitamin schedule, routine exercising, and appropriate, well-person physical examinations. An active lifestyle is the norm.

Intellectual

Proactivity in intellectual health refers to establishing a routine of research and preparedness in both the content and processes that have been proven to be effective in one's profession. Intentional leaders not only subscribe to professional journals, they also read them. When attending conferences, they have a mindset for learning and a self-promise to share their new knowledge with others when they return. Demonstrated enthusiasm for understanding not only serves the leader, it also fosters a pervasive climate of intellectual curiosity in the organization.

Emotional

Leaders at this level ensure their emotional well-being by making certain to schedule those persons and activities in their lives that lift their sense of well being and prevent anxiety or self-doubt before they happen. They are not afraid to ask for help, vent, or process with friends about issues that are causing them internal conflict. Celebration, humor, and joy are staples in their emotional diets.

Scripts

> "How can we expand this experience to make us wiser in future realities?"
>
> "What do I need to do as a leader to enhance the capacity of my team to deal with the complexities of this problem?"

"To have more energy for this job, I'm committing myself to work out daily."

"I have grown more this year than any other."

Indicators

- The focus of professional development is on anticipating, illuminating, and responding to changes on the horizon.
- Climate surveys are a regular practice in order to determine the needs and wants of those in the organization.
- Invitations are extended to employees to attend seminars about organizational and personal wellness.
- Leaders really want to know how others are taking care of themselves and their stress levels.
- There is a commitment to knowing and understanding trends for potential impact on the organization and its people.

Inspirational Level: Holistic

This level is not divided into sections because it is about the interconnectedness of the mind, the body, and the emotions. The life of a holistic person is a container within which all three elements are blended. Leaders who are truly holistic in their approach to health are consciously aware of the dependence of one aspect upon the other. For example, they recognize that a persistent cold may indicate more than just a physical issue. They look within their emotions and intellect, in addition to the medicine cabinet, for remedies. Their priority is to determine the root causes of any health issue as opposed to responding to symptoms. James Allen said it best, "The mind is the master weaver of the inner garment of character and the outer garment of circumstance."[62]

The relationships and activities of inspired leaders are balanced and include opportunities for physical exercise, intellectual challenges, and positive interactions. A holistic leader sees, understands, and values the depth of diversity within a people and has the capacity to coalesce their healthful energy and virtues for a better world order.

Most significantly, a holistic leader's perspective on living includes accepting the reality that life holds a spectrum of experiences ranging from: sadness to joy; searching to knowing; sickness to health; seriousness to playfulness; insecurity to confidence and so on. Within each spectrum, holistic leaders remain true to themselves and yet continue to learn and grow.

Another way to describe the differences among the three levels in the Facet of Health is to use the words of Edith Wharton, American novelist, who said, "There are two ways of spreading light: to be the candle or the mirror that reflects it.[63]" Given that metaphor, one could say:

The resilient leader "burns the candle at both ends."

The proactive leader is judicious about the number and the nature of the candles he or she burns.

The holistic leader *IS* the light.

Scripts

"The Walk for the Cure is a great way we can do something for ourselves, serve others, and contribute to a higher good."

"I want to be my best in order to serve as a role model for employees and colleagues."

"It is so evident that this organization is a happy/fun and productive place to work."

"Around here, we work hard and play hard."

Indicators

- They are students of a holistic life personally and professionally.
- The leader sees possibilities even in the darkest of times.

- People are celebratory in their words and actions.
- Leaders keep a reserve of energy to expend on what has heart and meaning to them.
- The leader knows how and when to say no.
- Holistic leaders inspire others by virtue of the choices they make.

Spirit Mover: Balance

As a Spirit Mover, balance does not mean equal parts. Rather, it represents a healthy integration of the physical, intellectual and emotional dimensions of life. Such integration is the result of leaders intentionally working to achieve clarity about the value and merits of each dimension. Consequently, leaders neither ignore nor sacrifice one dimension in the service of the others. It is essential that leaders achieve their own inner harmony in order to create conditions that cultivate a similar sense of balance within their organizations.

Resilient leaders, because they have not prepared themselves for intellectual, physical, and emotional problems, are more vulnerable to sudden imbalances. Because proactive leaders have *readied* themselves to prevent problems in each of the three areas, they are less inclined than their resilient colleagues to experience health problems.

The holistic approach to health has the *greatest potential* for lasting stability in life. The leader readily recognizes the capacity of each of the dimensions to assist the others when necessary. The highest and longest lasting level of equilibrium is possible only when the leader acknowledges the significance of balancing physical, intellectual, and emotional components of health.

Professional dancers recognize that balance is an absolute prerequisite to rhythm and movement. In a similar way, leaders who wish to become the choreographers for the wellness of people and organizations they serve must first operate from a strong, stable base.

RSVP

In terms of your emotional, physical, and intellectual health, what decision could you make that would be life-changing? Don't procrastinate. Act on your decision before another day passes.

Quotation:

> *"A 'no' uttered from the deepest conviction is better than a 'yes' merely uttered to please, or what is worse, to avoid trouble."*[64]
> —Mohandas Mahatma Gandhi

Spirit Movers: Attributes for Transforming Leadership

Elaborated Rubric for the Facet of Health

Facet	Informed (Prepared Way)	Intentional (Purposeful Way)	Inspired (Passionate Way)
Health	Resilient	Proactive	Balanced
Standard: *The leader establishes a state of personal and/or organizational well being in the physical, intellectual, and emotional dimensions.*	The leader responds to health issues in an appropriate way. An impact on one dimension of health is seen as isolated from the other two.	The leader anticipates the possibility of health issues and initiates preventative measures. The leader examines data regarding the health of the organization and takes action.	The leader understands and values the integration of the three dimensions of health. The leader invests in creating an organizational culture that fosters and supports the well-being of its people.
The Spirit Mover Is Balance.	**Organizational Indicators:**	**Organizational Indicators:**	**Organizational Indicators:**
	• Solutions to health issues focus on symptoms versus root causes. • Quick fixes are the norm. • Discussions of health issues arise only after symptoms occur. • Problems are not ignored, but may not be dealt with in a timely fashion.	• Data is purposely gathered to determine the total well being within the organization. • Policies and practices support the findings. • There is a commitment to knowing and understanding trends.	• There is a conscious effort by the leader to model the integration of physical, emotional, and intellectual wellness. • The healthy culture is specifically referenced as a reason people want to work there. • Employees initiate health-focused programs.

Chapter 12

The Facet of Accountability

*"The ancient Romans had a tradition: whenever
one of their engineers constructed an arch, as the
capstone was hoisted into place, the engineer assumed
accountability for his work in the most profound
way possible: he stood under the arch."*[65]
—Michael Armstrong, Author

Standard: **The leader accepts responsibility for personal and organizational results.**

By dictionary definition, accountability refers to the "liability to be called on to render an account; the obligation to bear the consequences for failure to perform as expected." In order to be accountable to their own standards as well as those of the organization, effective leaders must know not only *for what* they are responsible, but also *to whom* they bear that responsibility. Job descriptions, strategic plans, long-range goals, and outcome statements are all examples articulating the "*what*" of one's job. Supervisors, constituents, colleagues, and self are among the many possibilities that could represent the "to whom" of responsibility. It is critical that leaders find and accept those positions compatible with their own personal and professional beliefs, goals, and talent. Regardless of the level, leaders must make conscious decisions about the purpose and worth of accountability.

Informed Level: Delegation

Upon acceptance of the role of leader, those at this level accept accountability as an inherent part of the job. They see it as synonymous with evaluation and judgment. Further, they consider the accountability process as a series of hoops they must jump through in order to retain their positions and continue with their "real" work. These leaders understand the mechanics of administering such tools as surveys, reports, inventories, spreadsheets, etc. Even though they are skilled in the requirements of the process, these leaders are not likely to dedicate a great deal of rigor to the work because they see it as an isolated series of tasks with no relevance to their mission.

When leaders feel no passion about their work, the potential for joy or fulfillment is consequently diminished. Therefore, when it comes to the accountability process, *informed level* leaders often choose delegation over ownership. They recognize that one of the rewards of promotion lies in the ability to entrust specific tasks to those who are most motivated to accomplish them.

Leaders at the *informed level* do not value the potential of accountability to serve as a platform from which to engage in serious discussions about the achievements and challenges of the organization.

Scripts:

"I told the planning committee to avoid this course of action, but they insisted."

"The results of the survey are available for anyone who wants to see them."

"This is a task I don't want my fingerprints on."

Indicators

- The value of knowing what's really going on is situational.
- All activities required for accountability purposes are completed.
- Positive results are always highly publicized.
- The leader delegates in order to distance him or herself from the outcomes in the event they may be negative.

Intentional Level: Ownership

At this level, the "ownership" of accountability is seen as a duty and is approached as such. The leader openly proclaims willingness to accept responsibility for the success or failure of his or her own work and of those he or she leads. Rigor and intentionality are brought to the activities in the process. References to the evaluation and its findings are used to inform future planning. The leader's willingness to "own" all responsibility, regardless of success or failure, is viewed as courageous and admirable by many in the organization, especially those who feel they may have been "thrown under the bus" in previous situations. Loyalty to others is a clear value.

Leaders in the "ownership" category should be aware that focusing exclusively on themselves as lightning rods for accountability can eventually discourage the enthusiasm and support of others. Without broader investment and involvement, the potential for learning and co-creation that accompany a more-inclusive accountability process are impossible.

The first two levels in this facet can be encapsulated in two familiar phrases. While the informed leader is inclined to "pass the buck," the intentional leader asserts, "The buck stops here."

Scripts:

"I own this problem."

"I will take responsibility for any decisions we make as long as they are evidence-based."

"This project is non-negotiable."

"It's my responsibility and I'll do it!"

Indicators

- Leaders appropriately take responsibility for their own actions.
- The leader owns decisions whether or not they were delegated to others.
- The leader will accept full responsibility for actions and decisions if they believe the greater good will be served.
- Individuals are frequently rewarded and acknowledged for good work.
- Leaders are magnets for those at the *informed level* who do not want to be accountable.

Inspired Level: Signature

Inspired leaders clearly understand accountability is the shared responsibility of everyone in the organization. In their comprehensive view, they include themselves among those to whom they must answer for their work.

Inspired leaders don't just accept accountability for the work of the organization; they embrace it. Though they are clear about their position as leader, they also understand that the quality of the organization will depend on *all* of the employees and the constituents they serve. Data gathering is seen as a challenging and important opportunity rather than a burden. These leaders welcome any information that can be helpful in accomplishing the vision of the organization, regardless of the source. They are committed to true collaboration and constantly seek to understand and articulate the relationship between greater inclusion and the achievement of the mission to be accomplished.

Pat Riley, a very successful coach in the National Basketball Association and prolific author on the subject of teamwork, states, "Each warrior wants to leave the mark of his will, his signature, on important acts he touches. This is not the voice of ego, but of the human spirit, rising up and declaring that it has something to contribute to the solution of the hardest problems, no matter how vexing."[66]

This leader is a passionate optimist who has no reservations about attaching his name to his work or that of his co-workers. The "signature" spoken of in the inspired level is not about celebrating or claiming the credit for an accomplishment, but rather a willingness to testify to and accept shared responsibility for the higher level of collective wisdom.

Perhaps the most famous signatures in U.S. history grace the bottom of our Declaration of Independence. So famous have the names on that document become that one of them, "John Hancock," has even become a synonym for the word signature.

Scripts

"Okay, so that didn't work out too well, what did we learn?"

"I'm proud that we received this award. It will mean that we can do the following to improve our work."

"I dropped the ball on this one and I'm sorry, but thanks to all of you for picking it up again for me. Let's go from here."

"Would you sign your name to it?"

Indicators

- The pronoun "we" is used most often when discussing progress toward established goals.
- Individual work is recognized as it relates to the broader mission of the organization.
- Criticism is gratefully accepted, even though it may reflect on them personally.
- Advancement of the organization's vision and mission over self-success is very evident.

Spirit Mover: Truth

In this facet, it is the quest for truth that moves the spirit from delegation to ownership and ultimately to signature. The proposition that truth was a spirit mover for the founding fathers is clearly stated in their own words, "We hold these truths to be self-evident." Leaders who literally or figuratively co-sign their work as a testimonial to its validity set a powerful, symbolic precedent for others to follow.

When a leader agrees to share the quest for truth with others, regardless of the topic, that leader is agreeing to give up a portion of his or her individual power in order to benefit from more sources of interpretation. In return for sharing power, the leader is able to find a broader truth than that which he or she could find in isolation. In order to do this, the leader becomes a "truth seeker." The truths they seek might include:

- the truth about what makes us defensive
- the truth of what works and does not work

- the truth of what employees and customers do not know
- the truth about effectiveness and ineffectiveness
- the truth about motivations and intentions that drive decisions and actions
- the truth of what elevates the human spirit rather than robbing the soul
- the truth about the realities of change and its demands

Leaders need to model truth telling, and this demands listening, confronting false assumptions, objectivity, openness, vulnerability, and patience.

In addition to seeking and telling the truth, leaders must also *be* true to the closely held beliefs that comprise their personal ethics. This is a basic requirement for behaving with integrity. At the *inspired level*, the consistency between the leader's personal code of ethics and that of the organization are aligned to a high degree. Such compatibility allows the leader to readily affix his "signature" to the work at hand.

RSVP

Reflect on your role as a leader. If there were a signing ceremony describing your professional mission, what would be the title of the document? Type it. Print it. Frame it. Keep it where you can see it every day.

Quotation:

"There is not a truth existing which I fear...or would wish unknown to the whole world."[67]

—Thomas Jefferson, 3rd U. S. President

Spirit Movers: Attributes for Transforming Leadership

Elaborated Rubric for the Facet of Accountability

FACET	Informed (Prepared Way)	Intentional (Purposeful Way)	Inspired (Passionate Way)
Accountability	Delegation	Ownership	Signature
Standard: *The leader accepts responsibility for personal and organizational results.*	The leader is accountable to herself for her job and reputation. The leader occasionally transfers accountability for organizational results to others.	The leader accepts responsibility for her own work and the performance of those she leads.	The leader embraces accountability as integral to leadership and expects others to put their "signature" on their work. She is passionate about gathering information on the organization's performance and using it to improve.
The Spirit Mover Is *Truth*.	Organizational Indicators:	Organizational Indicators:	Organizational Indicators:
	• Negative results are attributed to the performance of others. • Delegation is sometimes used to avoid responsibility and/or tasks that are not of interest to the leader. • Assignment of responsibilities is often based on the competence and interest of others.	• Organizational performance is ultimately the responsibility of the leader. • Individuals and teams are publically rewarded for good work. • Poor performance is owned by leadership.	• Feedback in all forms on the work of the organization is welcomed, including criticism of the leader. • People willingly share responsibility for the results of their co-creations. • Accountability is a routine part of organizational improvement.

Chapter 13

Integrating the Facets

Thus far the facets in the rubric have been discussed in isolation for the sake of clarity. But of course, real life is never tidy or so easily compartmentalized. In this chapter several examples of the way facets can and have been integrated in the process of leadership are offered.

Talent/Vision

Just as a dance would make no sense without choreography, so a gifted leader with no vision would lead people in circles. The spirit mover of passion must combine with that of courage in order to reach a preferred destination. For example, Dr. Condoleezza Rice, former U.S. Secretary of State is also an accomplished musician, having studied as a concert pianist at the Aspen Music School. But she may have chosen to pursue a career in politics because it represented the best combination of her talent and her passion.

Time/Health

The demands on a leader's time are endless. Far too often, even the most effective leaders function at the *informed level* with regard to their health. Consumed by professional challenges, they become reactive. Their attention to physical, intellectual, and emotional needs becomes a priority only when the failure to do so causes them to become ill, unhappy, or disheartened. It is essential that leaders call upon the Spirit Movers of Discernment and Balance within the Facets of Time and Health in order to achieve a consistently holistic and soul-fulfilling life. Exercise, reflection, and spiritual renewal mark the calendars of balanced leaders.

The following standards serve as concrete examples of ways to articulate expectations about the wise use of time and health within an organization.

1. Employees are aware that every entry initiated on the calendar throughout the organization represents an investment of others' time and energy, and this investment is managed with care, trust, and wisdom.
2. Employees believe that positive, trusting relationships are critical to a safe and healthy environment and are willing to share the time and space necessary to build them.
3. Employees use open-mindedness and ingenuity to overcome the barriers imposed by conventional thinking about time.

The above standards are examples of what is possible when people have deeper conversations about the facets and how they can be integrated.

Change/Decision Making

The theory of chaos gave birth to the term "Butterfly Effect" used to describe the phenomenon whereby a small change at one place in a complex system has large effects elsewhere. It is said a butterfly flapping its wings in Rio de Janeiro might change the weather in Chicago. This phenomenon, when applied to organizational leadership, explains the inevitable relationship between the facets of change and decision making. In an era when participatory governance is valued (e.g., W. Edwards Deming's work on Total Quality Management), the impetus for change can come from anywhere in an organization. When a decision is made to implement a change in one part of the system, it will inevitably impact other parts of the same system. Subsequently, responses to those changes lead to further decisions and so the ripple effect continues. Though the time necessary and complexity of a participatory process is challenging, a humble leader recognizes that a broader base of input will result in a better decision.

Vision/Voice/Motivation

The previous three examples illustrated the interweaving of two facets but there are often more than two involved. We would like to show an example of three facets that often come together. They are Vision, Voice, and Motivation.

For example, consider the journey of Mohandas Gandhi (aka Mahatma Gandhi). An Indian lawyer, educated in Great Britain, he held a clear and historic vision of an India independent of foreign domination. He used his voice to involve the people of India in deeper discussions of the importance of nonviolence, truth, and passive resistance as weapons more powerful than traditional armaments. He was successful in motivating hundreds of thousands of people to form a covenant that ultimately resulted in India's independence. Although he was assassinated in 1948 his voice endures in his writings and in the voices of those who continue to study the powerful lessons found in his leadership legacy.

The absence or moderation of any of the three facets, Vision, Voice, and/or Motivation, would almost certainly have resulted in the unraveling of Gandhi's mission. Contrast the *informed level* (first level of our rubric) in these three categories with the tenets of Gandhi. It becomes obvious to the reader that Gandhi would not have been successful if he had been performing at that level. Informed leaders are motivated by rules and regulations while Gandhi believed in civil disobedience through passive resistance to what he felt were tyrannical laws. His voice, as opposed to being an internal dialogue, was a constant conversation with the Indian people, using whatever available media, including newspapers, radio, one-on-one discussions with world leaders, and informal conversations with the people. The historic nature of Gandhi's vision is clear in both its length (decades) and its breadth (an entire nation).

In this chapter, we have offered just a few illustrations of the exponential increase in complexity that occurs when multiple facets of leadership unfold in the natural resolution of a leadership challenge. We encourage readers to reflect on situations in which they've been called upon to integrate the facets of their leadership in order to resolve an issue or attain a goal.

Chapter 14

The Leader As Weaver

"If we are to achieve a richer culture, rich in contrasting values, we must recognize the whole gamut of human potentialities, and so weave a less arbitrary social fabric, one in which each diverse human gift will find a fitting place."[68]
—Margaret Mead

I n the preceding chapters, we have taken the phenomenon of leadership and delineated ten component facets. We then explored Spirit Movers, the energy forces that generate mobility from one level to the next. This *deductive* process served to help us analyze leadership by disassembling the elements within it.

This chapter seeks to use the reverse method, *induction*, to reassemble our leadership model into its broadest perspective. We wish to move from the finite and literal to the unbounded and figurative by presenting an artistic view to summarize our work.

We have chosen the fine art of weaving as our metaphor for leadership. In this extended comparison, the essence of the leader is personified by the weaver; the loom represents the rubric; the frame signifies the unique circumstances within which the leader must function; the Facets correspond to the threads; and the shuttle is the symbol for the Spirit Movers. The ultimate tapestry represents the total body of work the leaders have created throughout their tenure in leadership. It is their legacy.

The Weaver

Every weaver is unique. Each brings to the loom his or her singular essence. The influences on a leader's essence as described in chapter 1 hold true for weavers as well. For example, the influences of culture are clearly seen by contrasting bright, abstract, contemporary Native American tapestries with the more subdued, pictorial wall hangings from the past that were used to commemorate historical events. A weaver is clear about the purpose for performing his or her craft. While one may be driven by the need to sell her work for profit, another may be creating art for art's sake. Some are able to do both. Each leader must be clear about the essence and intentionality he or she brings to the loom (the table) before he can begin to create a unique leadership pattern to offer any organization.

The Loom

The weaver's loom parallels the "Rubric for Transforming Leadership" found at the end of chapter 2. It serves as the container in which the essential components of the book are held.

A loom is basically a lattice with both vertical and horizontal dimensions upon which a tapestry is built. A rubric is also a grid that contains aspects of length (the number of Facets) and depth (the *levels* within them).

Just as a weaver chooses the loom over other potential media such as painting, or sculpture, to express his/her art, we have chosen a rubric as a vehicle to convey our beliefs about leadership.

The Frame

The frame of a leadership loom signifies the circumstances within which the leader operates and his or her story unfolds. The sides of the frame will be defined by elements such as mission, vision, goals, constituency, history, and structure of the organization. Experienced weavers know from the onset of their work that it is difficult to make significant adjustments to the frame after the weaving has begun. A weaver can make some modifications to create new images within the desired pattern as the work unfolds. But the prospects of reconstructing the entire frame are not likely. For this reason, it is imperative for a leader to examine the "frame" of an organization to be certain the fabric of his leadership can be developed within it.

The Threads

Each of the Facets in our rubric corresponds to a strand of thread. Gifted weavers are purposeful about the materials they choose. The strength of the fiber will affect the durability of the fabric. Also, the choice of color and texture will determine the level of artistic merit.

Similarly, leaders, working to realize a vision, must be both strong and artful as they go about their work. The level of their development on each of the Facets of leadership will determine the quality of the repertoire of skills from which they will draw.

The Shuttle

Even when the loom, frame, and threads have been assembled, it is impossible for weaving to take place without a shuttle. This device, which is designed to be moved back and forth among the fibers, binding them in the desired pattern, is the symbol for the Spirit Movers. Of course, the shuttle in and of itself is worthless until it is moved by the spirit of the weaver. Only then does the inanimate object come alive. Great leaders are, indeed, spirit movers.

Knowledge of the facets and levels of leadership is insufficient to lead. It is only when the leader reaches within his core to grasp and apply the forces of *trust, love, presence, courage, passion, optimism, discernment, humility, balance, and truth* that he can move his own spirit and the spirits of those he or she leads. In the leadership rubric it is the Spirit Movers that convert potential into action and elevate the leader to greatness. Just as the frame and threads of a loom are inert until the weaver passes the shuttle among them, so leadership skills and understandings remain stagnant until the leader employs the Spirit Movers to propel him to higher levels.

The Tapestry

We view leadership as a singular, irreplaceable work of art, woven by the unique individual with whom the shuttle has been entrusted. With it in their hands, leaders answer the question, "What will you do with what you now know?" Their answers to that question result in their legacy.

As Sandra Day O'Connor said, *"We don't accomplish anything in this world alone… and whatever happens is the result of the whole tapestry of one's life and the weavings of individual threads."*[69]

Influencers

In our endnotes, as in most books, we acknowledge the published writings of those whose words have been directly quoted or paraphrased in the text of the book. We believe the gifts we have received from the following persons extend beyond specific wording or authorship. Their passion and ideas have been sources of reflection over time. They have subsequently been integrated into our thinking and have influenced our writing in ways both significant and seamless.

Elliot Asp: Consultant & Colleague
Maya Angelou: Author, Poet
Angeles Arrien: Author
Warren Bennis: Author
Peter Block: Author
William F. Bridges: Author & Mentor
E. Grady Brogue: Author
Alan Brown and Gail Chadwick; Mentors and Colleagues
Marcus Buckingham: Author
Leo Buscaglia: Author
Curt Coffman: Author & Advisor
Jim Collins: Author
Stephen Covey: Author
Terry E. Deal and Lee G. Bolman: Authors & Colleagues
Max DePree: Author
Peter Drucker: Author
Elliot Eisner: Patron of the Arts
Michael Fullan: Author

Howard Gardner: Author
Robert Greenleaf: Author
Margaret Hatcher: Author, Poet, Artist, Colleague
Gay Hendricks: Author
Craig Hickman: Author
Mary Jarvis: Consultant & Colleague
Rosabeth Moss Kanter: Author
John P. Kotter: Author
James M. Kouzes and Barry Z. Posner: Authors
Stephanie Pace Marshall: Author, Colleague
Parker J. Palmer: Author
Miguel Ruiz: Author
Robert D. Tschirki, PhD: Mentor & Colleague
Margaret Wheatley: Author

About the Authors

Cile Chavez, Ed.D

Cile Chavez, President of Cile Chavez Consulting, Inc. is a nationally and internationally recognized consultant and motivational speaker on leadership. She specializes in helping people and organizations realize, develop, and celebrate their potential in order to achieve worthy goals. Her expertise is grounded in her leadership and management roles in higher education as assistant dean of a college of education, deputy and superintendent of a metropolitan public school district, and as a board member/trustee of multiple public institutions and community foundations.

Dr. Chavez's clients have included over seventy-five state and national professional associations, State Farm Ins., IBM,

Hewlett-Packard, U.S. West, the U.S. Department of Defense Dependent Schools, AT&T, YMCA, and Andavo Corporate Travel. Her influence extends beyond the continental United States to Brazil, Singapore, the Philippines, Japan, England, and the United Arab Emirates.

Spirit Movers: Attributes for Transforming Leadership presently serves as a "container" for what she knows and understands about leadership after forty years of a professional career.

Julie Reder Fairley

Julie Fairley is an educator, author, speaker, and consultant who seeks to kindle both the mind and the heart.

Educator: Julie's career journey in educational leadership has extended from the classroom, to the office of the principal, to central administration. She has also taught master's level courses in Leadership Studies.

Author: Ms. Fairley has published two books on the topic of leadership: *Perpetual Notions: Parables about Leadership* (1987) and *Character Capsules: Leadership in Small Doses* (1997). She has also authored animated cartoon scripts for international audiences.

Speaker: Numerous presentations at state, national, and international conferences have afforded Julie opportunities to offer her voice as far away as China, Italy, Greece, and Ireland

and as near as neighborhood schools. Leadership, Change Management, and motivation are the primary areas of focus in her presentations.

Consultant: As the proprietor of Coachlight, LLC, Julie counts multiple public and private organizations among her clients.

Coachlight is named for persons in history who carried torches beside carriages travelling at night. They worked to shed light on the journeys of those they served.

Julie Fairley offers her co-authorship of *Spirit Movers: Attributes for Transforming Leadership* in the same spirit of service. (Additional information available at JulieFairley.com.)

Endnotes

1   "Guillaume Apollinaire quotes," ThinkExist.com Quotations Online 1 Aug. 2009, http://einstein/quotes/guillaume_apollinaire/ (Accessed 12 Sep. 2009)

2   Hatcher, Margaret. *The Healer Archetype Fieldbook: Practices and Resources for Personal and Professional Leadership*. Flagstaff, Arizona: Northern Arizona University, 2002. Page 3.

3   The Holy Bible, Matthew 26:41 (King James Version).

4   DePree, Max. *Leadership Is an Art*. New York: Doubleday, 1989. Page 9

5   "Rensis Likert quotes," ThinkExist.com Quotations Online 1 Aug. 2009.http://einstein/quotes/rensis_likert/ (Accessed Sept 15, 2009)

6   Axelrod, Alan. *When the Buck Stops with You: Harry S. Truman on Leadership*. New York: Penguin Group, 2004.Page 102.

7   Hatcher, Margaret. *The Teacher Archetype Fieldbook: Practices and Resources for Personal and Professional Leadership*. Flagstaff, Arizona: Northern Arizona University, 2003. Page 17.

8   Kouzes, James M., and Barry Z. Posner. *The Leadership Challenge*. San Francisco: Jossey-Bass, 1995. Page 167.

9   Heathfield, Susan, "Inspirational Quotations for Business and Work: Trust and Trustworthiness," *About.com*, http://humanresources.about.com/od/inspirationalquotations/a/trust.htm (Accessed June 12, 2009)

10   Lee, Blaine. *The Power Principle: Influence with Honor*. New York: Fireside Publishers, 1997. Page 272.

11   Covey, Stephen. *Principle-Centered Leadership*. New York: Simon & Schuster, 1990. Page 259.

12   Roosevelt, Franklin Delano. *First Inaugural Address*, March 4, 1933. http://historymatters.gmu.edu/d/5057/

13   "Lao Tzu quotes," *ThinkExist.com Quotations Online*, 1 Aug. 2009. http://thinkexist.com/quotation/being_deeply_loved_by_someone_gives_you_strength/9115.html (Accessed 10 Aug. 2009)

14   Baldwin, James Arthur. *The Fire Next Time*. New York: Vintage Books, 1993. Page 95.

15   Saint-Exupéry, Antoine de. *The Little Prince*. New York: Harcourt, Brace and World, 1943. Page 70.

16   Stravinsky, Igor. *Igor Stravinsky—An Autobiography*. New York: W. W. Norton & Co., 1998. Page 81.

17   Kleiser, Grenville. *Dictionary of Proverbs*. New Delhi: A. P. H. Publishing, 2005. Page 97.

18   "Buddha quotes," *ThinkExist.com Quotations Online*, 1 Aug. 2009. http://einstein/quotes/buddha/ (Accessed 18 Sep. 2009)

19   Jackson, Phil, with Hugh Delehanty. *Sacred Hoops: Spiritual Lessons of a Hardwood Warrior*. New York: Hyperion. 1995. Page 52.

20   Canfield, Jack, et al. *Chicken Soup for the Soul of Couples*. Deerfield Beach, FL; Health Communications Inc., 1999. Page 60.

21   Kegley, Charles Jr., and Shannon L. Blanton. *World Politics: Trends and Transformations*. Boston: Wadsworth Cengage Learning, 2009. Page 562.

22   Mother Theresa. *Meditations from a Simple Path*. New York: Ballantine Books, 1996. Page 61.

23   Kumar, Satish, and Freddie Whitefield. *Visionaries: The 20th Century's 100 Most Influential Leaders*. White River Junction, VT: Chelsey Green Publishing, 2007. Page 17.

24   Chitkara, M. G. *Consumerism, Crime and Corruption*. New Delhi; A. P. H. Publishing, 1998. Page 51.

25   Stevenson, Robert Louis. *The Works of Robert Louis Stevenson, Vol. 4, Vailima Ed*. New York: C. Scribner's Sons; etc. 1921. Page 315.

26   Marshall, Stephanie. *The Power to Transform: Leadership that Brings Learning and Schooling to Life*. San Francisco: Jossey Bass, 2006. Page 204.

27   Andrews, Robert. *Famous Lines: A Columbia Dictionary of Familiar Quotations*. New York: Columbia University Press, 1997. Page 67.

28   Tolle, Eckhart. *The Power of Now: A Guide to Spiritual Enlightenment.*
      Novato, CA: New World Library, 2004. Page 229.

29   "Rev. Theodore Hesburgh quotes," *World of Quotes,* http://www.
      worldofquotes.com/author/Theodore-Hesburgh/1/index.html
      (Accessed Oct. 9, 2008)

30   Kennedy, Robert. "Robert Kennedy Speeches," http://www.bobby-
      kennedy.com/rfkspeeches.htm (Accessed March 2, 2007)

31   Buckingham, Marcus. *The One Thing You Need to Know: about Great
      Managing, Great Leading, and Sustained Individual Success.* New York:
      Free Press, 2005. Page 59.

32   Maginn, Michael D. *Managing in Times of Change: 24 Lessons for Leading
      Individuals and Teams.* New York: McGraw Hill Company, Inc., 2009.
      Page 3.

33   Gladwell, Malcolm. *The Tipping Point: How Little Things Can Make a
      Big Difference.* New York: Little, Brown & Company, 2002.

34   Shakespeare, William. (*Julius Caesar*). *Bartlett's Familiar Quotations.*
      Boston: Little, Brown & Company Limited, 1885. Page 217.

35   Gide, Andrew, and David Littlejohn. *The Andrew Gide Reader.* New
      York: Knopf Publishing, 1971. Page 187.

36   Kennedy, John Fitzgerald. *Profiles in Courage.* New York: Blackdog and
      Leventhal Publishers, 1955. Page 255.

37   King, Dr. Martin Luther, Martin Luther King, Jr., and James M.
      Washington (Editor*). I Have a Dream: Writings and Speeches that Changed
      the World.* New York: Harper Collins Publishers, 1986. Page 104.

38   Mannion, Annemarie. "Rotarians in Action," *The Rotarian*: Feb. 2008,
      Volume 186, Page 18.

39   Obama, Barack. "Address at Cairo University, Egypt." June 4, 2009

40   "Leo Buscaglia Quotes," Brainy Quotes, http://www.brainyquote.com/
      quotes/quotes/l/leobuscagl150305.html (Accessed Feb. 22, 2008)

41   Adler, Mortimer Jerome, and Max Weismann, Editor. *How to Think
      About the Great Ideas from the Great Books of Western Civilization.* Peru,
      Illinois: Open Court Publishing, 2000. Page 117.

42 "Marshal Ferdinand Foch quotes," ThinkExist.com Quotations Online. 1 Aug. 2009, http://einstein/quotes/marshal_ferdinand_foch/ (Accessed Jan. 19, 2008)

43 Coffman, Curt, and Gabriel Gonzalez Molina, Ph.D. *Follow This Path: How the World's Greatest Organizations Drive Growth by Unleashing Human Potential.* New York: Time Warner Book Group, 2002. Page 103.

44 Ramsey, Robert D. *What Matters Most for School Leaders.* Thousand Oaks, CA: Corwin, 2005. Page 54.

45 Dole, Elizabeth. *Hearts Touched with Fire: My 500 Favorite Inspirational Quotations.* New York: Carroll and Graf, 2004. Page 146.

46 Wheatley, Margaret. *Turning to One Another: Simple Conversations to Restore Hope to the Future.* San Francisco: Berrett-Koehler Publishers Inc., 2002. Page 27.

47 Bell, Chip R. *Managers as Mentors: Building Partnerships for Learning.* San Francisco: Berrett-Koehler Publishers, 2002. Page 125.

48 Kanter, Rosabeth Moss. *The Change Masters: Innovation and Entrepreneurship in the American Corporation.* New York: Simon & Schuster, 1983. Page 13.

49 Buckingham, Marcus. *The One Thing You Need to Know: about Great Managing, Great Leading, and Sustained Individual Success.* New York: Free Press, 2005. Page145.

50 Ehrmann, Max. *Desiderata.* Kansas City: Andrews McMeel Publishers, 2003. Page 5.

51 Forbes, Charles B. *Forbes Magazine.* Vol. 136. 1985, Page 18.

52 Powell, Colin. *My American Journey.* New York: The Random House Ballantine Publishing Group: 1996. Page 335.

53 Chang, Larry, Editor. *Wisdom for the Soul: Five Millennia of Prescriptions for Spiritual Healing.* Washington, DC: Gnosophia Publishers, 2006. Page 707.

54 Neustad, Richard, and Ernest R. May. *Thinking in Time: The Uses of History for Decision Making* New York: Free Press, 1988.

55 Wood, Gordon S. *The Purpose of the Past: Reflections on the Uses of History.* New York: Penguin Books, 2008. Page 71. 1909.

56   Bryan, William Jennings. *Speeches of William Jennings Bryan: Revised and Arranged by Himself.* New York: Funk & Wagnalls Co., 1909.

57   Boswell, James. *Boswell's Life of Johnson.* New York: Charles Scribner's Sons, 1917. Page xviii.

58   Drucker, Peter Ferdinand. *Classic Drucker: essential wisdom of Peter Drucker from the pages of Harvard Business Review.* Boston: Harvard Business Press, 2006. Page 120.

59   Wheatley, Margaret. *Finding Our Way: Leadership for an Uncertain Time.* San Francisco: Berrett Koehler Publishers, 2005. Page 184.

60   Franklin, Benjamin. *Poor Richard's Almanac Orig. Printing 1733.* New York: Barnes & Noble Publishers, 2004. Page 29.

61   Disraeli, Benjamin. Speech, July 24, 1877, in *Bartlett's Familiar Quotations.* Boston: Little, Brown & Company Limited, 1885. Page 502.

62   Allen, James. *As a Man Thinketh.* Radford, VA: Wilder Publications, 2007. Page 7.

63   "Edith Wharton Quotes," *ThinkExist.com Quotations Online,* 1 Aug. 2009.   http://en.thinkexist.com/quotation/there_are_two_ways_of_spreading_light-to_be_the/204236.html (Accessed 18 Sep. 2009)

64   Anderson, Peggy. *Great Quotes from Great Leaders* (Gandhi, Mohandas Mahatma.).Illinois: Great Quotations Publishing Co., 1990. Page 83.

65   *Encarta Book of Quotations,* Swainson, Bill, and Microsoft. New York: St. Martin's Press. 2000. Page 34.

66   Riley, Pat . *The Winner Within: A life plan for team players.* New York: Putnam Books, 1993. Page 268.

67   "Fear Quotes and Proverbs: Thomas Jefferson Quotes," *Heart Quotes,* http://www.heartquotes.net/fear.html (Accessed March 15, 2008)

68   "Margaret Mead," *Wikiquote,* http://en.wikiquote.org/wiki/Margaret_Mead (Accessed April 10, 2009)

69   Jone Johnson Lewis, "Sandra Day O'Connor Quotes," *About.com,* http://womenshistory.about.com/od/quotes/a/s_d_oconnor.htm   (Accessed September 19, 2009)

Please Note

We gratefully acknowledge the enrichment the words of others add to the original core of this book. All quotations used herein remain the intellectual property of their respective originators, and we do not assert any claim of copyright for individual quotations. All use of quotations is done under the fair use copyright principle.

CPSIA information can be obtained
at www.ICGtesting.com
Printed in the USA
LVOW11s1816160617
538407LV00001B/110/P